KRIS YAO ARTECH | 姚仁喜 大元 建築工場

SECTION
KRIS YAO | ARTECH

Kris Yao, Hon. FAIA

Photo taken by Barry Lam, Founder and CEO of Quanta Computer.

Many years ago, when I was just starting to practice architecture, I had a sudden epiphany on a classical Chinese term that I had learned since childhood. "*Tang ao*" (堂奥)—two simple syllables—encompasses everything about the act of creating architecture. *Tang*, in the literal sense, means the room, the hall, or the space one sees upon entering through an open door. *Ao*, its counterpart, refers to what cannot be seen, yet can be sensed and mentally constructed through the context of *tang*. *Tang* and *ao* therefore represent the seen and the unseen. Importantly however, what is unseen is not the same as non-existent; it just exists in a different dimension. Despite this simplicity, it took many years of practicing architecture for me to truly appreciate the profundity embedded within these two words.

Of course, *tang ao* signifies something much deeper than their literal meaning. Everything that we find meaningful possesses this dual quality, and architecture is no exception. The physical presence is obvious and tangible, while the emotional aspect is intangible, ambiguous, and often mysterious. And in architecture, both aspects are equally important and inseparable. Without *ao*, architecture becomes pure technology—a mere feat of engineering; and without *tang*, there is no physical basis to contextualize a deeper form of communication, . *Tang* and *ao* are like the two wings of a bird that, when balanced, allow it to soar. The challenge of achieving this balance is what makes architecture so complex and so fascinating. Architects create places by working with the limitations of inanimate objects—brick, stone, wood, concrete, glass—yet we strive to create limitless meanings and memories of these places for those who inhabit them.

Tang ao also has a cinematic quality. It captures a sense of space–time progression, a sequence, an exploration. The contrast between a Western painting and a Chinese scroll painting provides a good analogy for this concept. The former presents an image that is clear, decisive, and frozen in time, whereas the latter is akin to watching a film: as the scroll is unfurled at one end, and rewound at the other, slowly revealing its contents, a procession of impressions accumulate to construct a composite mental image. Likewise, when we move through the spaces of a building, *ao* can become *tang* as we anticipate what lies ahead, then encounter the expected (or the unexpected), with each new experience adding to the previous.

For many of the projects in this book, the attempt to investigate both aspects—the tangible and the intangible—provided one of our main challenges, and this was particularly true for the

culture projects. The practical brief for Wuzhen Theatre, for instance, was to create two interconnected, flexible, modern performance spaces, but we were also keen to reflect the atmosphere of its Jiangnan water-town location. Recycled building materials, such as old ship timbers, handcrafted city-wall bricks, and clay roof tiles, were therefore chosen to capture the sense of a bygone era and to complement this uniquely preserved historic site, free from modern materials and means of construction.

At the Water-Moon Monastery, banners fluttering in the wind, sunlight entering the interior through walls hollowed out with scriptures, and reflections of various kinds create the sense of an illusory and ephemeral space, in response to the Buddhist master client's suggestion that the monastery reflect the notion of "moon in the water, flower in the sky."

In our recently completed New Taipei Art Museum, a labyrinth of slowly ascending paths, made from chiseled concrete and local brick, echo the atmosphere of the narrow streets in the nearby old town. These contrast with the rectangular art museum that hovers above, clad with randomly patterned aluminum panels and sandblasted metal pipes—designed to create phosphenes, and inspired by the reeds that grow abundantly in and around the site.

Even in commercial projects, whenever possible, we try to transform the usual experience by creating dramatic spatial elements. One example is the Eslite Suzhou. In this bookstore and shopping mall complex, rather than the usual atriums and escalators, visitors are greeted in the entry by a sunlit grand stairway flanked by a gigantic architectural concrete wall, leading from the first to the third floor. Since its opening, the complex has become the perfect stage-set for selfie-lovers, and the most visited commercial complex in the area.

Of course, it would be naive to expect that visitors will always perceive an architect's vision exactly as intended; in reality, the original intention and the final reception often have startlingly little in common. Nevertheless, architects must persist in trying to create what they believe will be meaningful spaces for those who use them, which is why a profound understanding of human psychology and appreciation of a particular location's history, culture, and natural environment is so crucial.

SECTION: KRIS YAO|ARTECH is our fifth monograph, after 38 years of practice. It presents a cross-section of major projects spanning a decade—2012 to 2023—across a variety of different building types. We also celebrate our obsession with architectural sections by including these for most entries, to illustrate our spatial intentions and highlight recurring motifs. Looking back over past work is something I never find easy, but the very purpose of a monograph is to do just that, and I hope that the process of reflecting on what we have produced over the last ten years will help realign us for future challenges.

At KYA, we're fortunate to be able to work on projects of all kinds, from commercial complexes to cultural venues, and from secluded sites to urban centers. Rather than restricting ourselves to any particular specialism, we instead try to apply the "beginner's mind"— always attempting to see a project with fresh eyes, and constantly reminding ourselves of the great Zen master Shunryu Suzuki's words: *"In the beginner's mind there are many possibilities, but in the expert's mind there are few."* And we are lucky that, rather than considering us as experts in possession of a specific formula, our clients trust our professionalism and appreciate our sense of curiosity, enabling us to create thoughtful, sensible spaces, with them and for them.

We believe that the places we build should be continually adaptable and sustainable, and have positive transformative power, creating meaningful experiences for people. Despite our human limitations and the day-to-day challenges we face, I've always found encouragement in these words from the ancient Greek ephebic oath: *"I shall not leave my land any less but rather greater than it was left to me."*

A parable by the great ancient Chinese philosopher Zhuangzi tells the story of three emperors: *Shu*, the emperor of the North Sea; *Hu*, the emperor of the South Sea; and a feature-less, direction-less being called *Hundun* who rules over the central kingdom (Literally, *Hundun* means "paradox", "obscure", or "primordial chaos". In fact, the Chaos theory of modern quantum physics is translated as "Hundun theory" in Chinese). *Shu* and *Hu* (interestingly, the two names combined means "in an instant", "in the very moment") admired and appreciated *Hundun* very much, but they think his featurelessness is a problem for them to solve, so as a friendly and gracious gesture, *Shu* and *Hu* decided to carve out eyes, ears, nostrils and mouth for him, creating one of the seven sense openings each day. After seven days, when all the features are complete, *Hundun* dies.

I find this so profoundly symbolic to what we do as architects—or anyone who creates things in a spirit of optimism—that it is worthwhile to reflect upon. We try to make order out of chaos, we build with good intentions for

a better future, but most likely, we lose whatever we have come forth for because the order that we so hang on to is nothing but, to quote Einstein, an admittedly tenacious illusion*. What Zhuangzi tells us is that our instantaneous habit to fix things with dualistic thoughts and logical manipulation can often quickly kill intuition and mystery that stem from primordial purity. Therefore, by training ourselves to appreciate holistic, non-dual approaches, we may discover a world abundant with possibilities that require less effort.

And yet, as mortals, we have no choice but to maintain our optimism, to strive continuously to make sense of the unknown. We have to believe that what we do may create a better world for now and for the future—but always, with a healthy dose of humility.

* In a letter to his deceased friend Michele Besso and family, Einstein wrote: "…. For people like us who believe in physics, the separation between past, present and future has only the importance of an admittedly tenacious illusion."

FOREWORD

Michael Webb

Michael Webb is a Los Angeles-based writer who has authored more than twenty books on architecture and design, most recently Architects' Houses, and Building Community: New Apartment Architecture, while contributing essays to many more. He is also a regular contributor to leading journals in the United States and Europe. Growing up in London, he was an editor at The Times and Country Life, before moving to the US. He was awarded an honorary membership in the Los Angeles chapter of the American Institute of Architects, and made a Chevalier de l'Ordre des Arts et des Lettres for his services to French culture.

Water-Moon Monastery

From the serenity of a Buddhist monastery to the energy of a high-speed train station and the urbanity of a corporate headquarters, the architecture of Kris Yao is versatile and far-flung. KRIS YAO | ARTECH, the firm he established in 1985, has explored many typologies, while winning acclaim for a succession of museums, campuses, office towers, and cultural complexes in the past three decades. The scale has grown but the varied buildings are consistently fresh and original. "Every project is a brand-new experience and I need to feel the spirit of place," says Yao. "I take an intuitive rather than analytical approach, using very simple forms that conceal the complexities of each structure."

The twenty-seven new and recent projects in this monograph scattered across a vast geographic area, yet each is a distinctive response to program and context while sharing a common DNA. Architecture and nature are interwoven; even on dense urban sites, buildings often step back from the street behind a landscaped forecourt. Beyond the city centers, they

Foxconn Headquarters Shanghai

Hupan Center

take their cues from rivers and lakes, rocks and trees, echoing their fluid forms or offering the sharp-edged contrast of a machine in the garden.

In a succession of museums, Yao has created architectural promenades that draw visitors in from the point of arrival, revealing every aspect of the building and its displays as they turn and ascend. Each shift of direction or level discloses a new vista. Movement is choreographed to turn spectators into active participants and encourage them to make their own discoveries. As Yao explains, "I envisage architecture as though I were shooting a movie. Scene follows scene as the camera moves through the spaces, and I hope that visitors will share that experience and gather on the stage I have created."

Corporate towers are conceived as building blocks that enrich the urban fabric while serving as a symbol of identity for the owner. KYA's towers, from the shimmering facades of the China Development Headquarters in Taipei to the geometric complexity of Foxconn in Shanghai and China Steel in Kaohsiung, convey a sense of stability and purpose without resorting to the ponderous historicism or tortured shapes of so many commercial developments. Springy, elegant, and welcoming, they serve public and private interests in equal measure.

Yao's architectural thinking is infused with spirituality. One could describe him as a sage with a twinkle in his eye; discerning and reflective, with a firm grasp of practicalities. "Our inhibitions and suspicions block us from using our inherent wisdom," he observes. "Meditation is like a glass of muddy water; if you allow it to sit, the mud will subside and the water will clear; yet, in real life, we keep shaking it." That ability to view the transient world with calm deliberation translates into the stillness one encounters at the heart of his cultural and educational projects. They serve as refuges from the city, and oases of serenity amidst the frenzy of urban life. The new campus for

Palace Museum Southern Branch

Hupan Center is, literally and figuratively, an island on the land. A circular enclosure surrounded by a moat contains varied spaces for teaching and study, and a reception hall on a little island in the central lake. It refers back to the scholars' gardens of ancient China.

Yao feels very close to traditional Chinese culture and is an accomplished calligrapher. He describes his concept for the Palace Museum Southern Branch as being based on three calligraphic forms: a brushstroke using thick ink, another using half-dry ink, and a "smeared" stroke. The new internet headquarters is conceived as a hilltop village flanked by tea plantations and camphor groves outside the city of Xinchang. Small buildings abstract the regional vernacular of white walls and pitched tiled roofs, and they flank a central canal traversed by stepping stones. And the Wuzhen Theater is a fusion of new and old that mediates between a painstakingly restored water town on one side and the contemporary quarters beyond. Looking at KYA's body of work and the plenitude of awards, it's clear that the firm has enjoyed a fruitful dialogue with most of its clients. It has established itself as the most creative design force in Taiwan, raising the bar for its peers, developers, and institutions. It has also mastered the challenge of building in China, retaining control of its projects through the construction process to ensure a high level of execution. KYA can offer the solid foundation of a long-established practice and the fresh thinking of a much younger firm by fusing the best of the past culture with contemporary needs and technologies. Young architects have much to learn from Yao's reinterpretation of classic traditions and its emphasis on the importance of site, as well as local materials and practices. For KRIS YAO | ARTECH, the next three-decades may be even more productive than the first.

-Michael Webb

4	PREFACE	
16	FOREWORD	
22	CONTENTS	
	PROJECTS	

New Taipei City Art Museum	24
Palace Museum Southern Branch	38
Museum of Prehistory	52
Wuzhen Theater	66
Water-Moon Monastery	80
Feng Zikai Arts Center	94
Hefei Central Library	102
Taipei City Concert Hall and Library	112
TSMC Nanjing Campus	120
Hainan Energy Trading Building	134
Foxconn Headquarters Shanghai	146
Tong Hsing Electronics	160
TSMC Hsinchu R&D Center	170

China Development Headquarters	182
Joy City Chongqing	194
Far Eastern Retail Complex	206
United Daily News	216
Hua Nan Bank	228
A Hilltop Campus	238
Changhua High-Speed Rail Station	246
Hotel Resonance Taipei	256
Han-Gu Villa	268
Hotel Indigo Taipei	278
Cosmology Center Taiwan University	290
Hupan Center	304
Dharma Drum Institute of Liberal Arts	314
Han Pao-Teh Memorial Museum	330

340	**SELECTED PROJECTS**
346	**TEAM**
350	**CREDITS & GRATITUDE**

◀
Exterior view of the museum and the art village still under construction.

Client: Cultural Affairs Bureau, New Taipei City
Area: 32,420 m²

The New Taipei City Art Museum (NTCAM) sits between the old towns of Yingge and Sanshia, with Mount Guilin to the north, and the Dahan River and Xueshan mountain range to the south. The competition to design the museum was won with the concept of an "art museum among the reeds." The intention was to create an open and accessible display of art that was fully integrated into the landscape, housed in a building that also achieved a high level of sustainability. The design blends the natural and the fabricated, interpreting elements of one in the form of the other, and vice versa.

Museums in Taiwan often exclude those unable to afford the price of entry. The NTCAM compensates for this with a vast open-air concrete art village on the ground floor that is open to all. This network of "streets" and sculpture terraces has an angular geometry that recalls the patterns of cracked mud in the Dahan riverbed during the dry season, as well as the spatial organization of the old streets of Yingge and Sanshia. Visitors are free to wander around this sculpture park, exploring its artworks, cafés, and workshops.

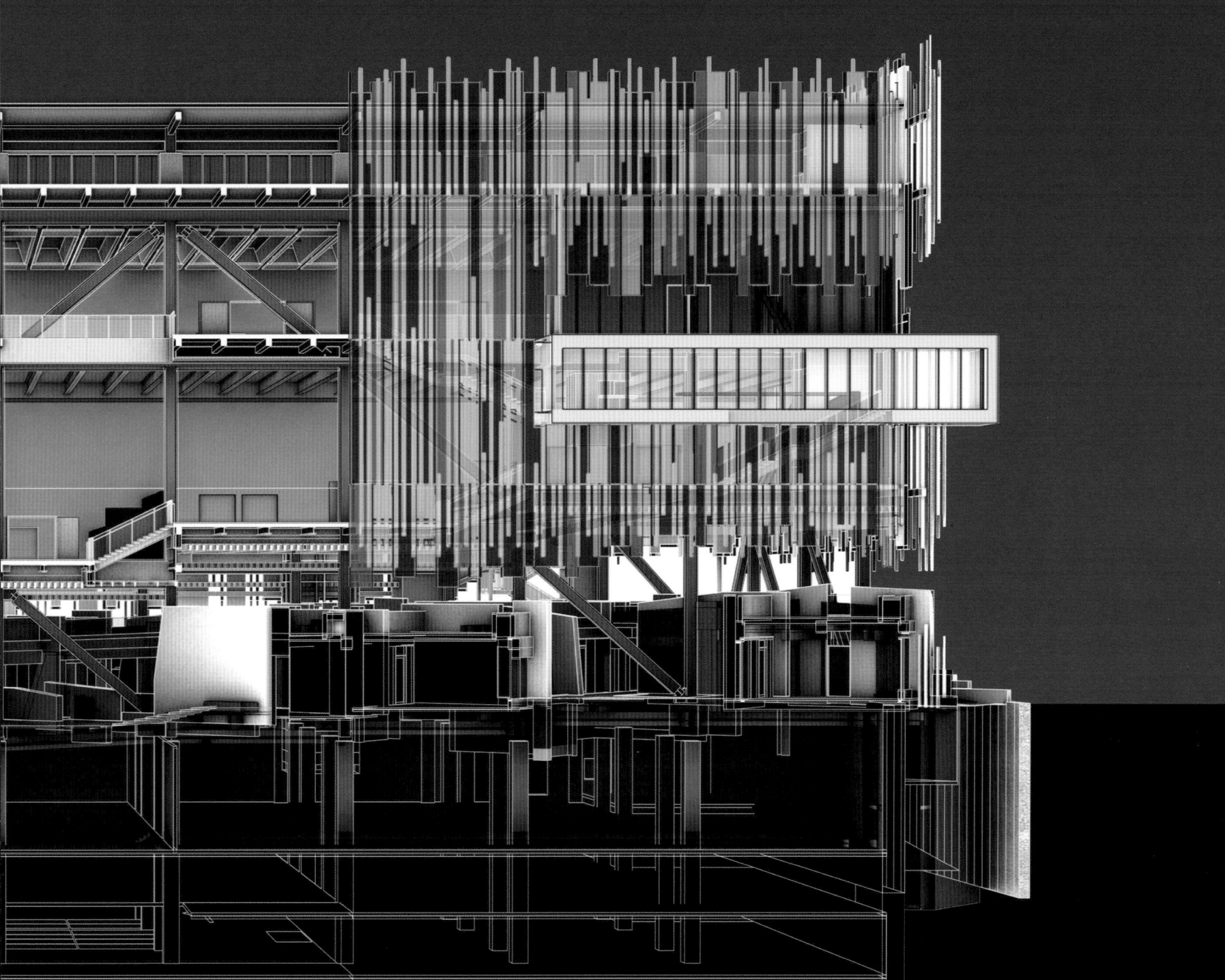

▲ Construction in progress, a close-up view showing the external stairs leading up to the museum.

▲ Construction in progress, the RC walls of the art village precede the museum to welcome and guide visitors in.

The 4.4-hectare site is located within a riverside art park in the Yingge District, with the Yingge Ceramics Museum and Sanying Art Village as its neighbors. Heading south from the Yingge train and MRT station, visitors find themselves at the top of the embankment that overlooks the site, with its existing reedbeds. A bridge provides direct access to the art village, which serves as an intermediate space between the exterior and the interior, the floors above and below, the museum and a performance hall, as well as the Dahan River and surrounding parkland. Visitors can choose to take an elevator to the exhibitions above, investigate the auditorium and children's museum below, or simply enjoy the relaxed atmosphere of the art village, enlivened with street-theater performances.

Clear views into the building's interior underscore the concept of a museum open to all, while also allowing it to coexist comfortably with the natural environment—a platform where conventional art, regional culture, and collective experience merge.

A long-span structural system elevates the main building mass above the site, ensuring an exhibition space that is as flexible as possible, and providing visitors with panoramic views of the river and mountains. Its facade is covered in a multitude of structural and nonstructural vertical steel tubes of varying lengths that reference the preexisting reedbeds; when seen from a distance, the tubes appear to sway like reeds in the breeze, obscuring the mass behind them. As with the Palace Museum Southern Branch,

this is a building that manages to stand out from the landscape while also enriching visitors' appreciation of that landscape. It is particularly notable for its harmonious scale, the integration of its open and enclosed areas, and the freshness of its architectural language.

▶
A close-up shot of the art village's RC wall showing the texture of its cross section, each chiseled by hand to create its own unique pattern.

Rendering of the art village during the competition stage.

A grand staircase brings visitors to the elevated lobby on the second floor, from where they can then access three floors of exhibition spaces, organized into four different types: general exhibition rooms, large-scale exhibition rooms, international exhibition rooms, and specially themed exhibition areas. A garden restaurant is located on the roof, where guests can enjoy an extensive view of the Dahan riverscape. And an additional noteworthy design feature is the individual circulation to the operation management center and the collection storage, which expedites control and security measures.

The structure of the museum consists of two parts: the upper portion, with large spans of column-free spaces catering for exhibition needs, and the ground-floor area, with a typical reinforced concrete beam-and-column construction. The facade is finished with rows of 35-centimeter-diameter steel tubes, with a structural column positioned almost imperceptibly between them every 3.6 meters. The Vierendeel trusses are also arranged at intervals of the same length to create an efficient and economical structural system that also provides many open spaces for electrical and mechanical facilities to pass through. The building's main stability and lateral force resistance system rely on the three reinforced concrete cores and the column-and-truss framework around the perimeter.

The nature and function of art museums continues to shift with the times, and there is always pressure on architecture to adapt to these evolving demands. In this instance, the NTCAM's art village rejects a typical designated circulation route in favor of allowing visitors to wander at their leisure. The art village and the building floating above it are also given the freedom to "speak" to each other, connected via a visual language that rejects barriers between interior and exterior, and between public and private, underscoring the concept of a vibrant, living space that is accessible to all.

▶ Construction in progress, the main exhibition hall on Level 6 that spans almost 100 meters in length.

▶ Construction in progress, the art village extends under the museum, accessible to all.

結構鋼管
Structural Steel Tube
遮陽鋼管(內含排水及機電管線)
Shading Steel Tube
(including drainage and MEP pipes)
粗糙表面之陶棒
Bar Terracotta with Bump Surface
兩層線紋玻璃構成之雙層牆系統
Double Wall System with Two Layers of Linear Patterned Glass
高效能膠合複層低輻射玻璃
High Performance Laminated IGU with Low-E Coating
LED燈管
LED Light Tube
沖孔鋁管
Perforated Aluminium
不鏽鋼管
Stainless Steel

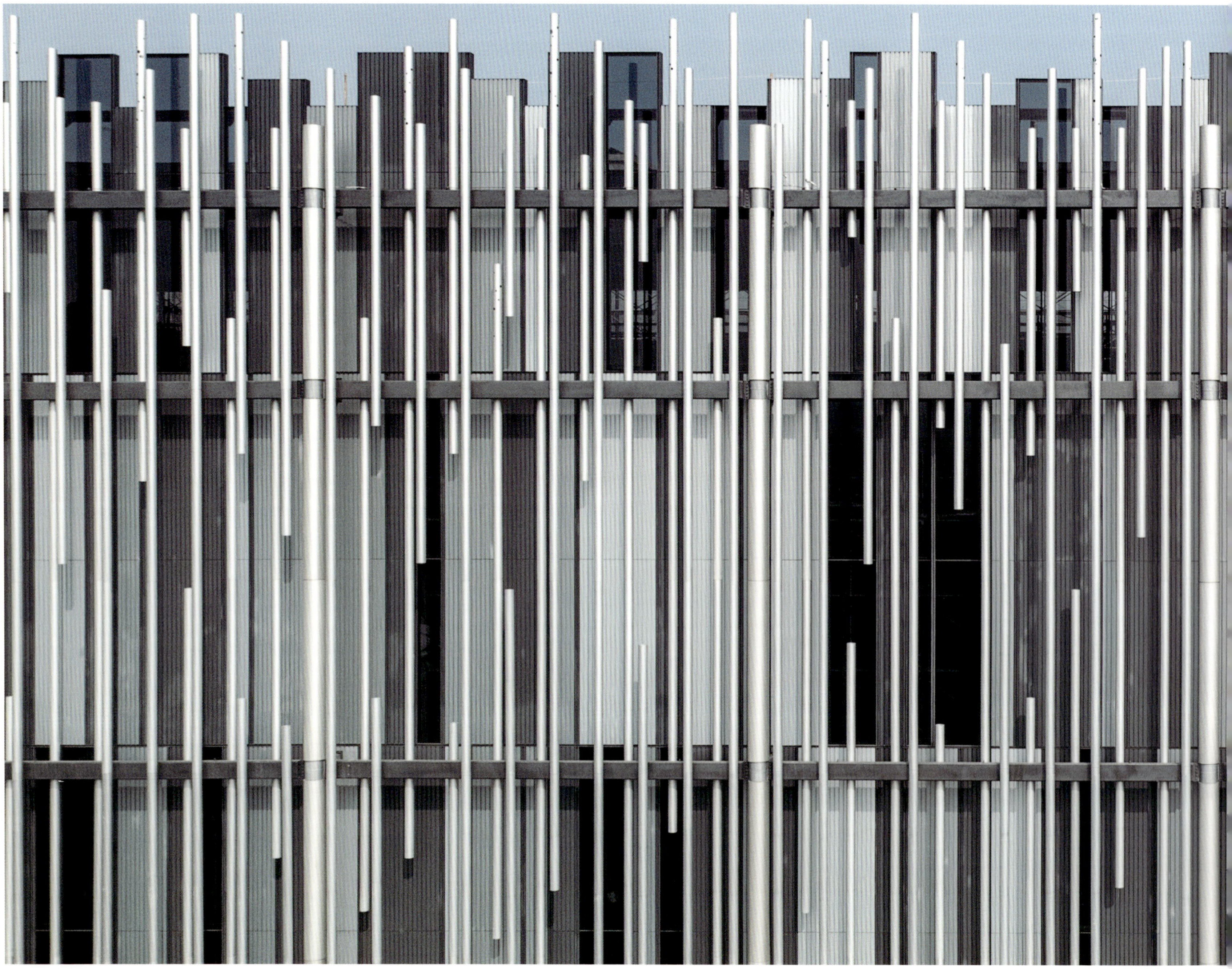

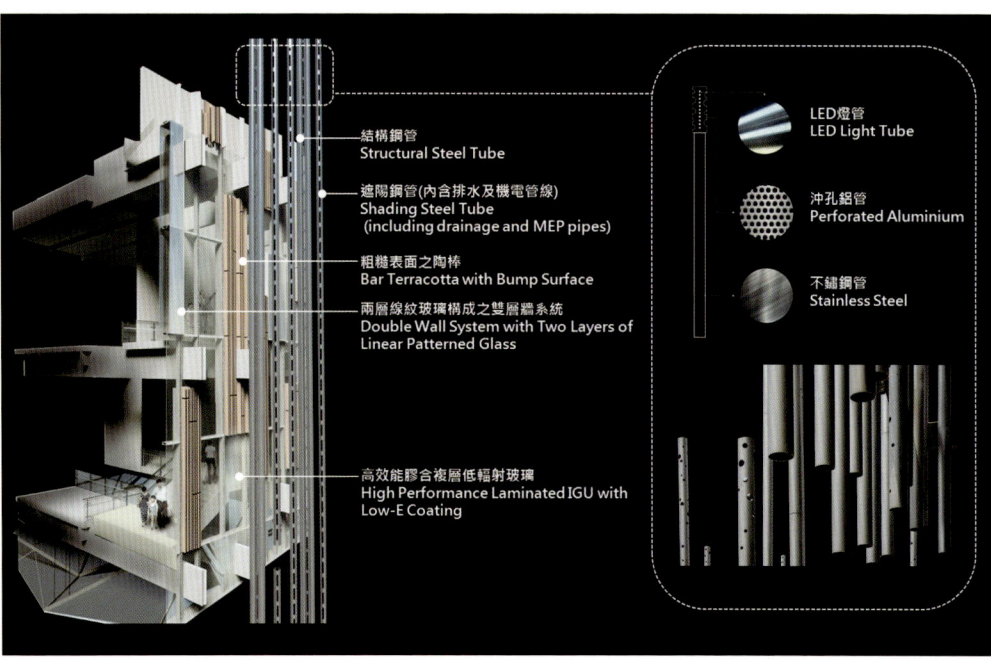

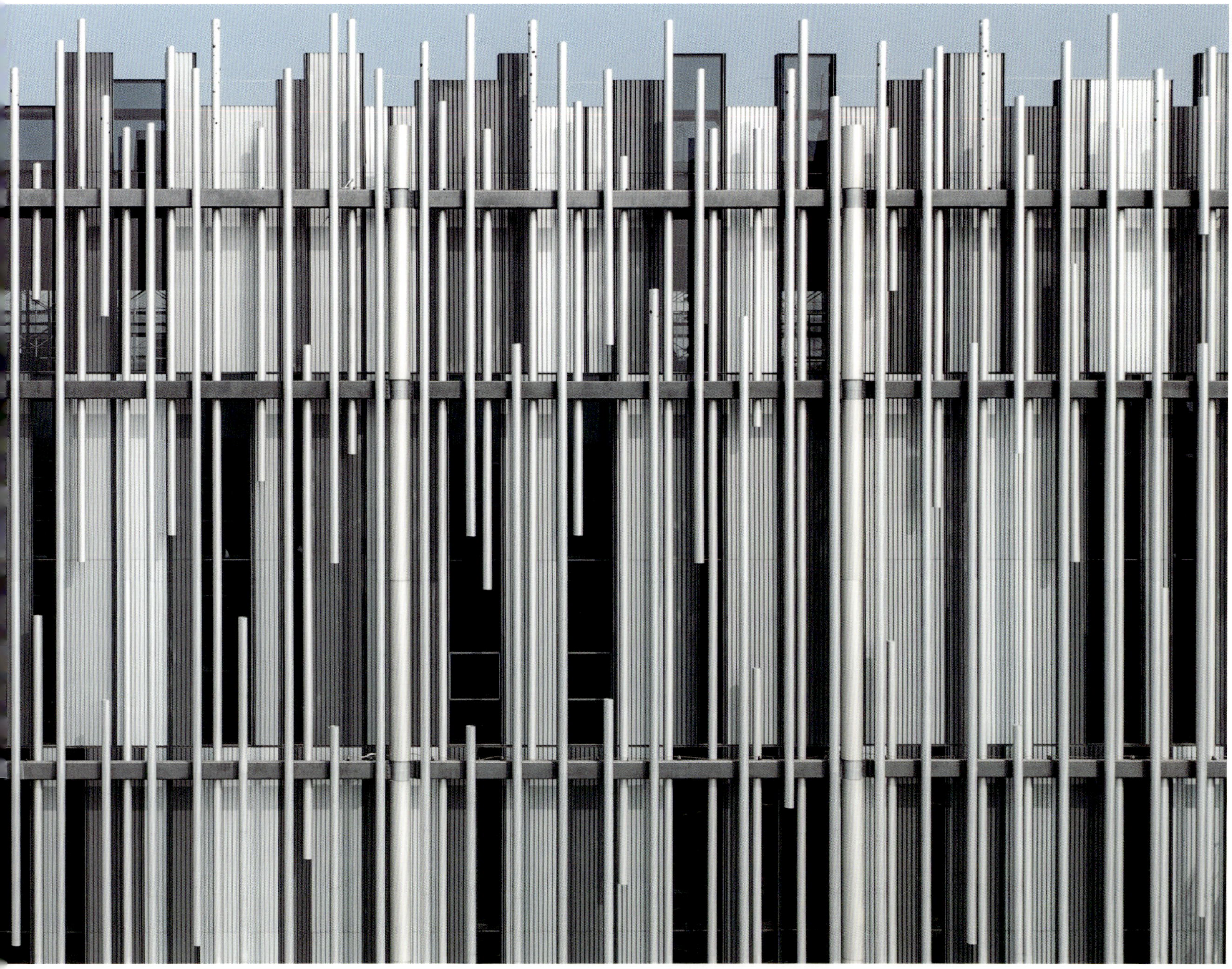

▶ Structural columns are camouflaged within rows of steel tubes on the facade. When the wind whips past these metal pipes, a symphony of the natural and the fabricated plays a melody unlike any we have heard before.

◀ The RC walls of the art village is casted in China Fir wood patterns.

◀ The China Fir wood panels as molds of the RC wall casts, each carefully selected to achieve a high-quality outcome.

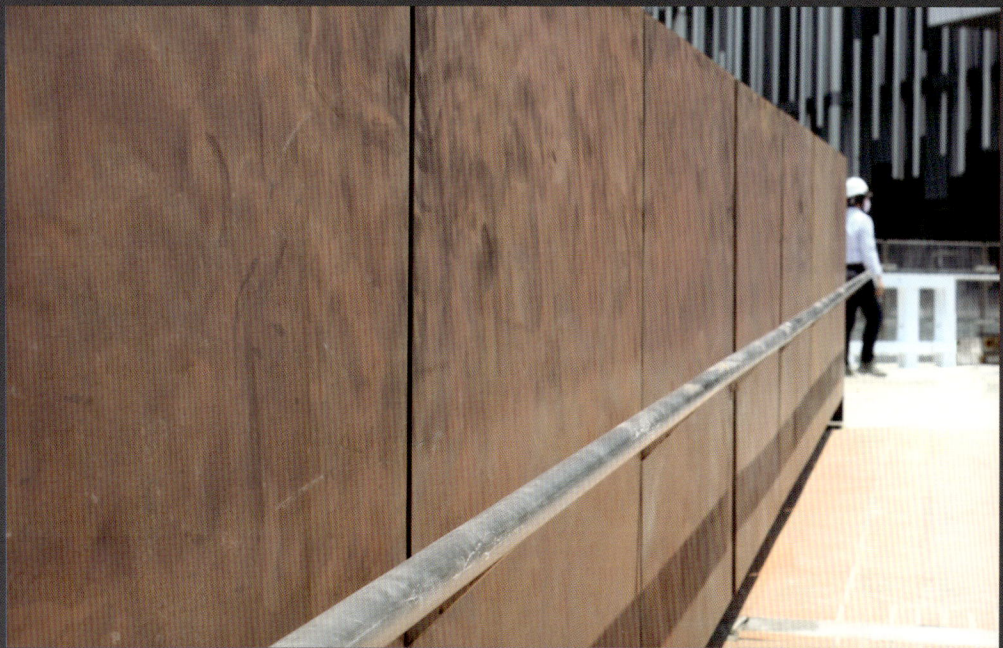

◀ Weathering steel panels on two sides of the arrival bridge.

PALACE MUSEUM SOUTHERN BRANCH

Completed year: 2015 | Location: Chiayi, Taiwan

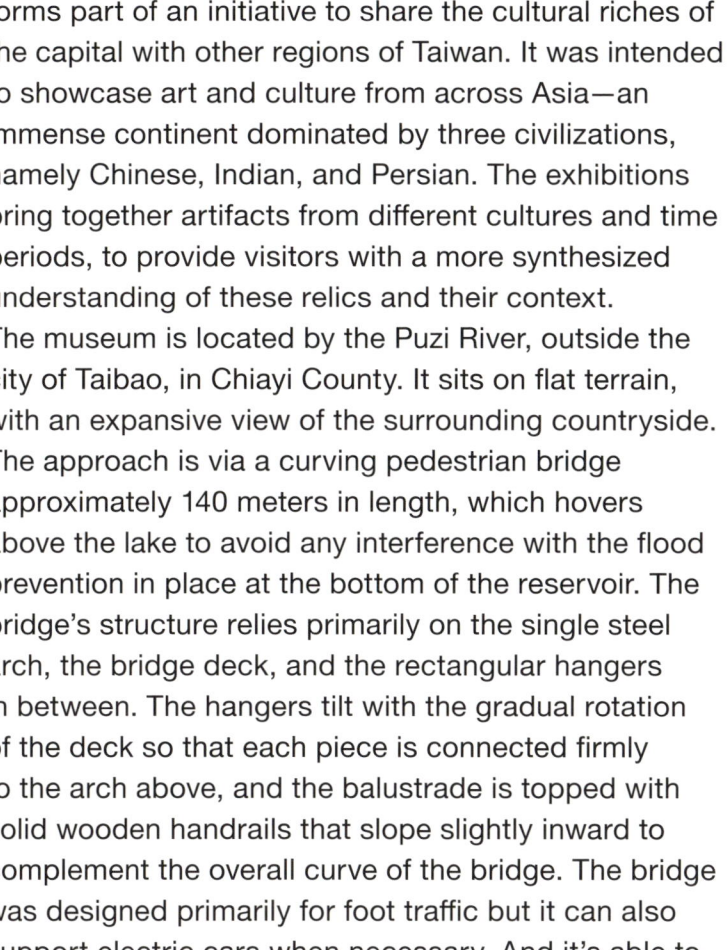

Client: National Palace Museum
Area: 38,332 m²

This ambitious satellite of Taipei's Palace Museum forms part of an initiative to share the cultural riches of the capital with other regions of Taiwan. It was intended to showcase art and culture from across Asia—an immense continent dominated by three civilizations, namely Chinese, Indian, and Persian. The exhibitions bring together artifacts from different cultures and time periods, to provide visitors with a more synthesized understanding of these relics and their context.
The museum is located by the Puzi River, outside the city of Taibao, in Chiayi County. It sits on flat terrain, with an expansive view of the surrounding countryside. The approach is via a curving pedestrian bridge approximately 140 meters in length, which hovers above the lake to avoid any interference with the flood prevention in place at the bottom of the reservoir. The bridge's structure relies primarily on the single steel arch, the bridge deck, and the rectangular hangers in between. The hangers tilt with the gradual rotation of the deck so that each piece is connected firmly to the arch above, and the balustrade is topped with solid wooden handrails that slope slightly inward to complement the overall curve of the bridge. The bridge was designed primarily for foot traffic but it can also support electric cars when necessary. And it's able to support large numbers of spectators on its deck on special occasions, when people assemble to watch fireworks or other events on the lake.

The design of the main building was inspired by Chinese calligraphic strokes—a "thick ink" stroke, combined with a "half-dry" stroke. The solid black thick-ink stroke in the west and the white half-dry void in the east collide at both ends of the curved volume. Toward the north, the black rises up and nudges into the white; at the opposite end, the white rises up and intersects the black. This collision of contrasting components is handled meticulously, resulting in a clean and congruous finish, as if they are two interlocking objects destined to come into contact with each other to form a whole.

The construction of the cantilevered spaces was a fun challenge to overcome. Forty-five temporary columns were put in place to support the protruding structure before the primary steel frames were completed. The moment of truth came when the supports had to be removed—followed by excitement as the structural design proved its excellence. The building now stands proudly and steadily in the beautiful greenery of the Chianan Plain.

The half-dry glass enclosure contains the museum lobby, café, library, and administrative offices. Supported by a steel structure and wrapped in light-gray low-E glass, the volume was kept transparent and well-lit to offer a welcoming public space that visitors can socialize and relax in. The steel frames protrude from the envelope to act as a vertical brise-soleil, deflecting some of the hot Chiayi sun, and the low-E glass combats the intense glare and heat gain from direct sunlight as well as indirect reflections off the lake. In the main lobby, the glass curtain wall frames striking views of the man-made lake and surrounding landscape. A grand stairway rises up gently, leading visitors to an orientation room where light-filled circulation spaces open into an inner courtyard and lead on to the softly lit exhibition galleries.

The thick-ink solid carapace protects light-sensitive artifacts in the curatorial department and exhibition halls. Making up the western half of the building, this black curved volume blocks the majority of the sun received by the building. Its exterior is clad in more than 36,000 cast aluminum disks attached to a gently bowed wall: a digitized version of an ancient bronzeware pattern. The disks were also deliberately placed so that as the sun moves, their reflections evoke the image of a dragon riding through the clouds.

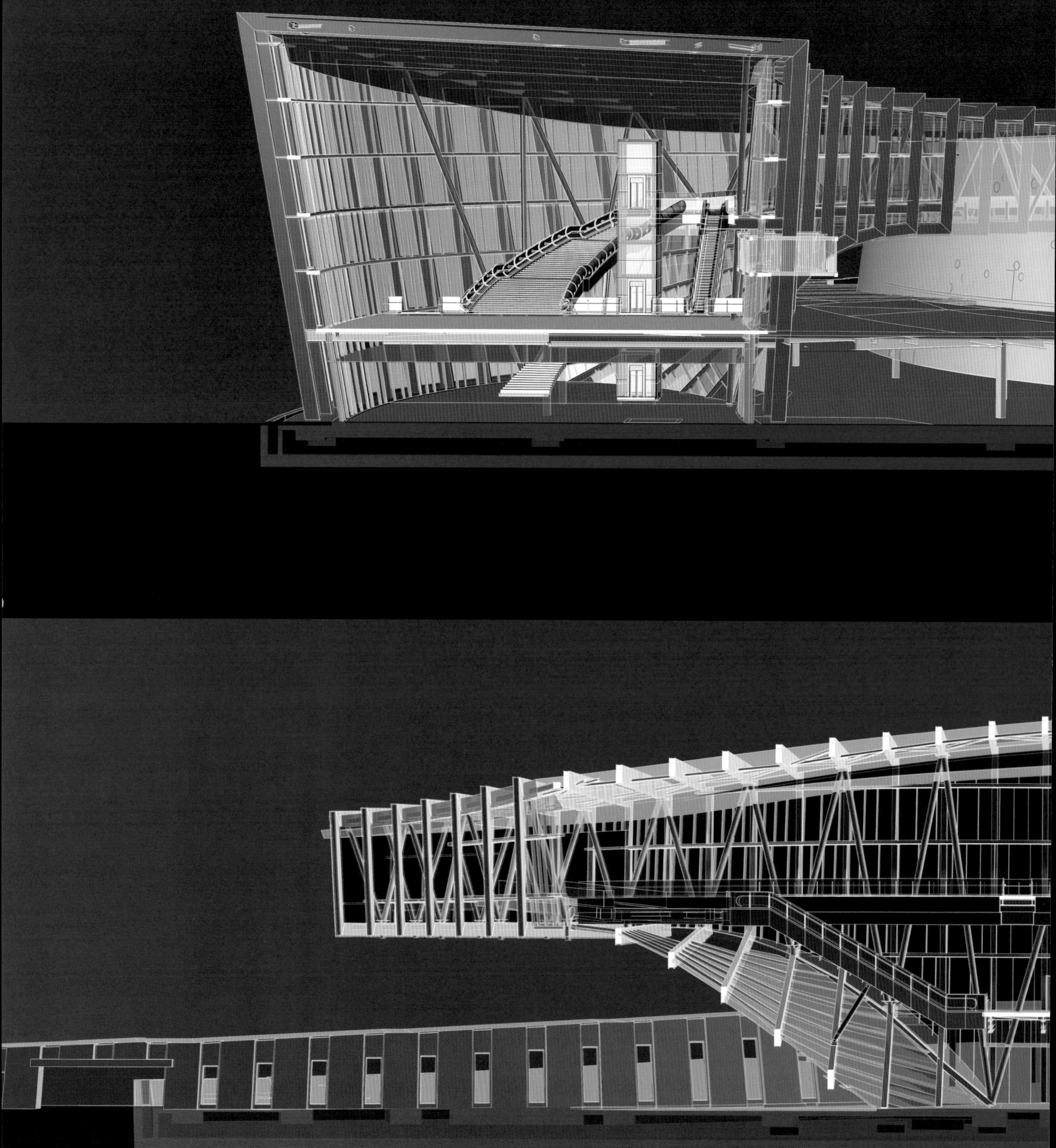

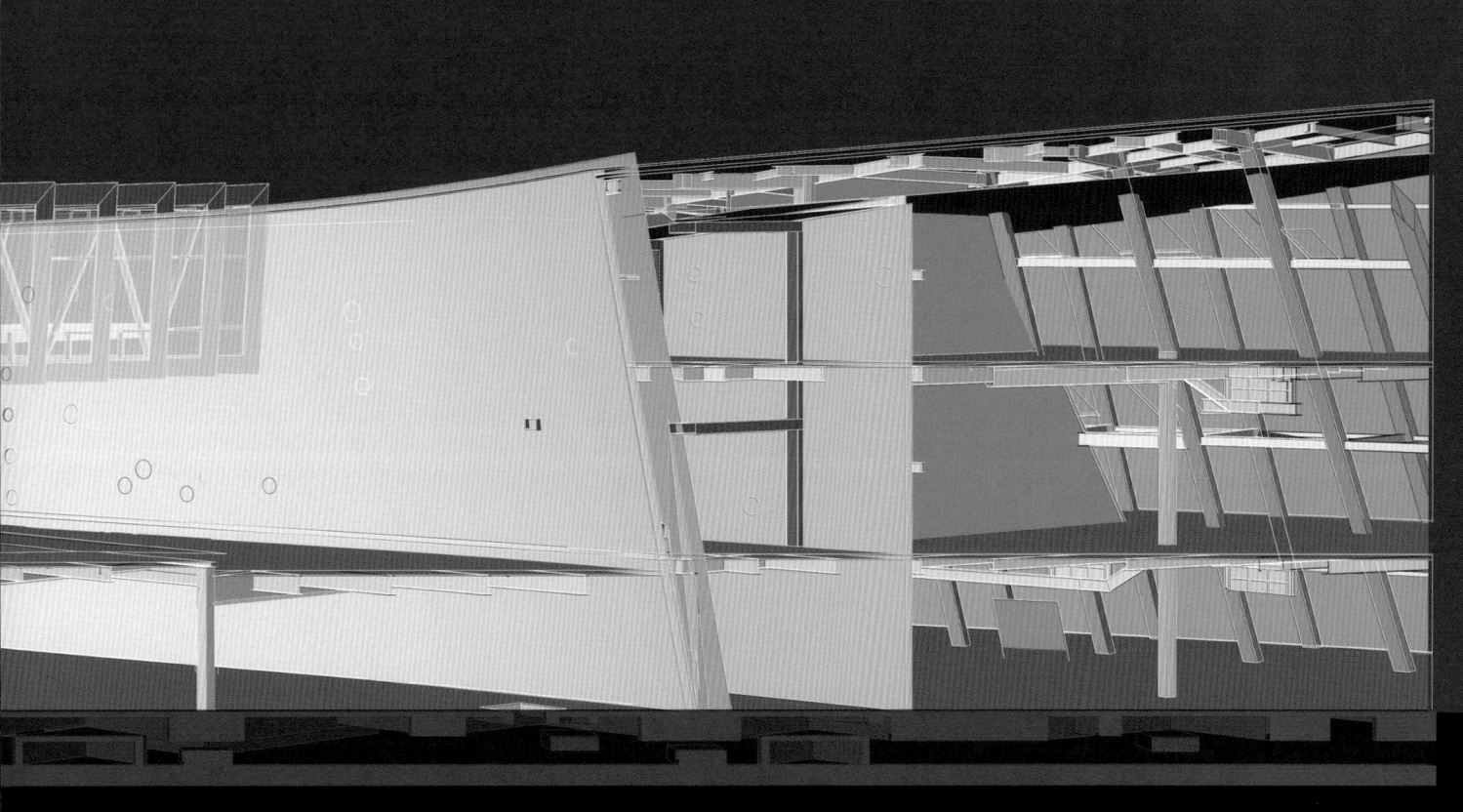

Short sectional perspective through the lobby (left) and the exhibition space (right).

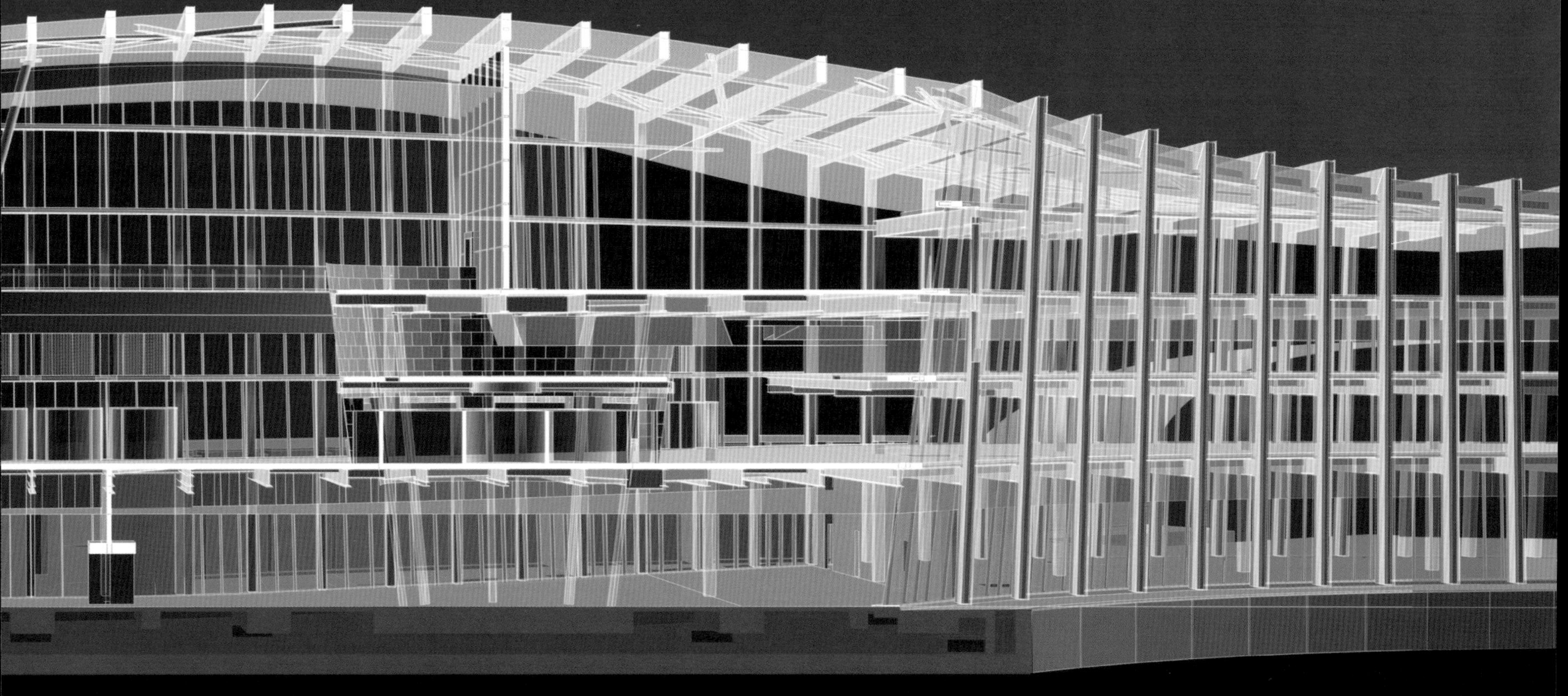

Long sectional perspective through the lobby.

Large openings were installed at both the northern and southern ends of the building to facilitate ventilation and bring in additional sunlight. The internal junction then performs as a threshold between the light public spaces and the dark exhibition rooms, placed at the beginning and end of the visitor's journey.

▶ Intersection of the glazed volume and the solid mass at the tip, creating a viewing platform from which to survey the beautiful Chianan Plain.

The area surrounding the museum takes the form of a miniature landscape, densely populated with a diverse selection of local species. Seen from a distance, the building appears to rise out of a billowing mass of vegetation—a setting that pays tribute to the abundant rainfall, sophisticated irrigation channels, and lush greenery of the region. The landscape design also captures the cultural heritage of the area, with motifs drawn from prehistoric times, as well as from the traditions of the Pingpu and Tsou people, scattered throughout. At night, the museum lights up gracefully like a beautiful waterside artwork, enhancing rather than disturbing the nighttime vista of Taibao City and its stunning surroundings.

MUSEUM OF PREHISTORY

Completed year: 2017　|　Location: Tainan, Taiwan

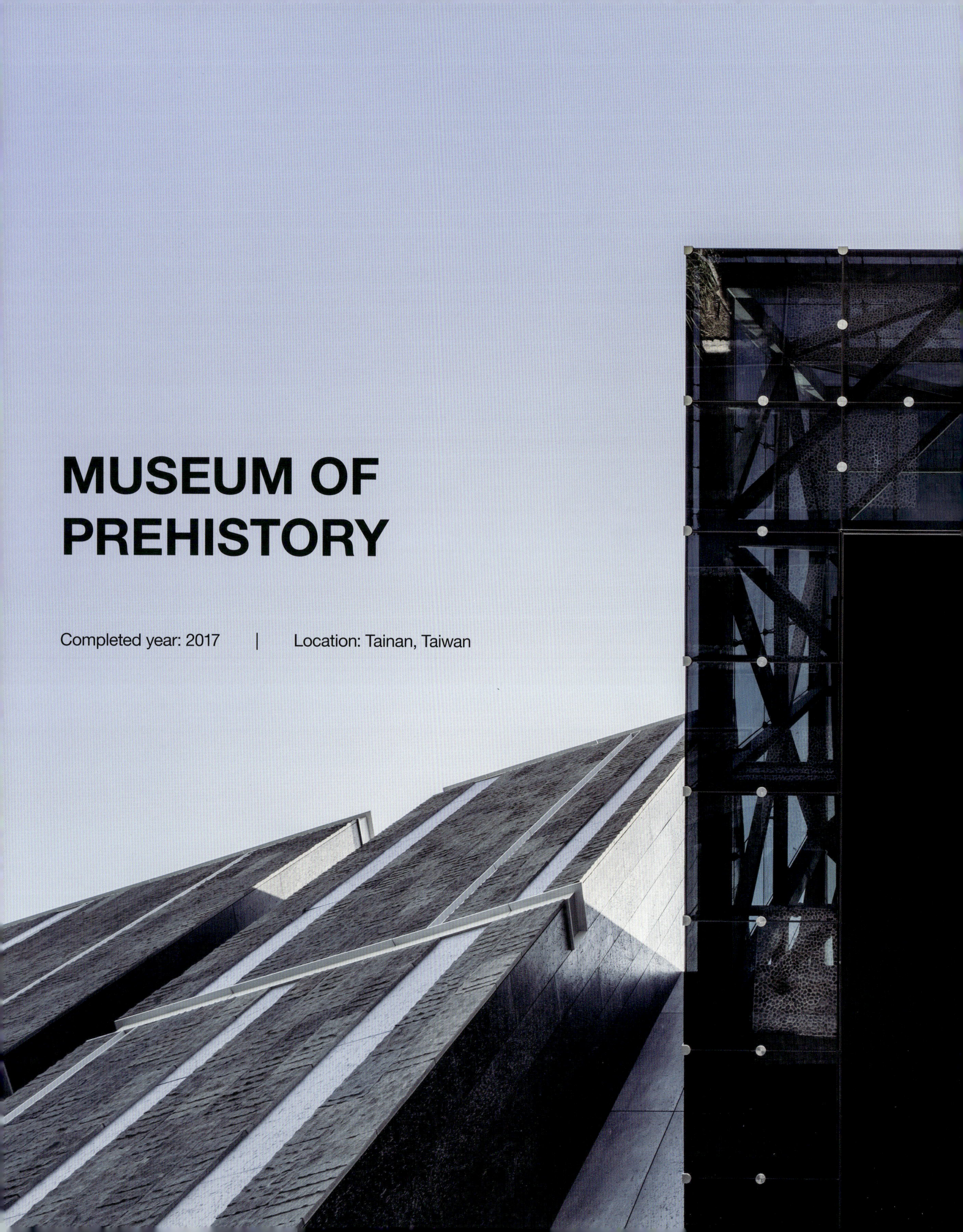

Client: National Museum of Prehistory
Area: 18,715 m²

The Museum of Prehistory sits in the Southern Taiwan Science Park, where relics dating back 5,000 years have been unearthed. The building follows two different axes. The first has a north-south configuration, and this takes the form of a black basalt block, pointing toward true north, in the manner of ancient burial sites, symbolizing the order of the past. The other axis rotates 19 degrees to align with present-day Tainan's city grid, and over this, a glass tube hovers, adhering to the order of the modern world. These twin concepts run through the entire museum, from the placement of the building itself to the display of objects, signifying the very nature of archaeological work—namely, using methods of the present to explore evidence of the past, and applying a modern perspective to interpret objects from a previous time.

▲
The lower end of the square glass tube juts out from the solid block and digs into the ground like a test probe.

The museum consists of three architectural elements. First is the square main building, each side being 70 meters long and 21 meters tall. Its surface is clad with split-face basalt, producing a black brutalist mass that sits stably on the site. Second is the monumental square tube, 90 meters in length and with a square section of 8.7 by 8.7 meters. This was constructed from structural glass wrapped around a series of steel frames. The glazed square tube slices the main building in half, dividing displays from offices, storage areas, and conservation labs, clearly splitting the space into one area for staff, and another for visitors. Third is the square aluminum section, each side measuring 3.3 meters wide, which runs externally from floor to floor, tying the two other elements together.

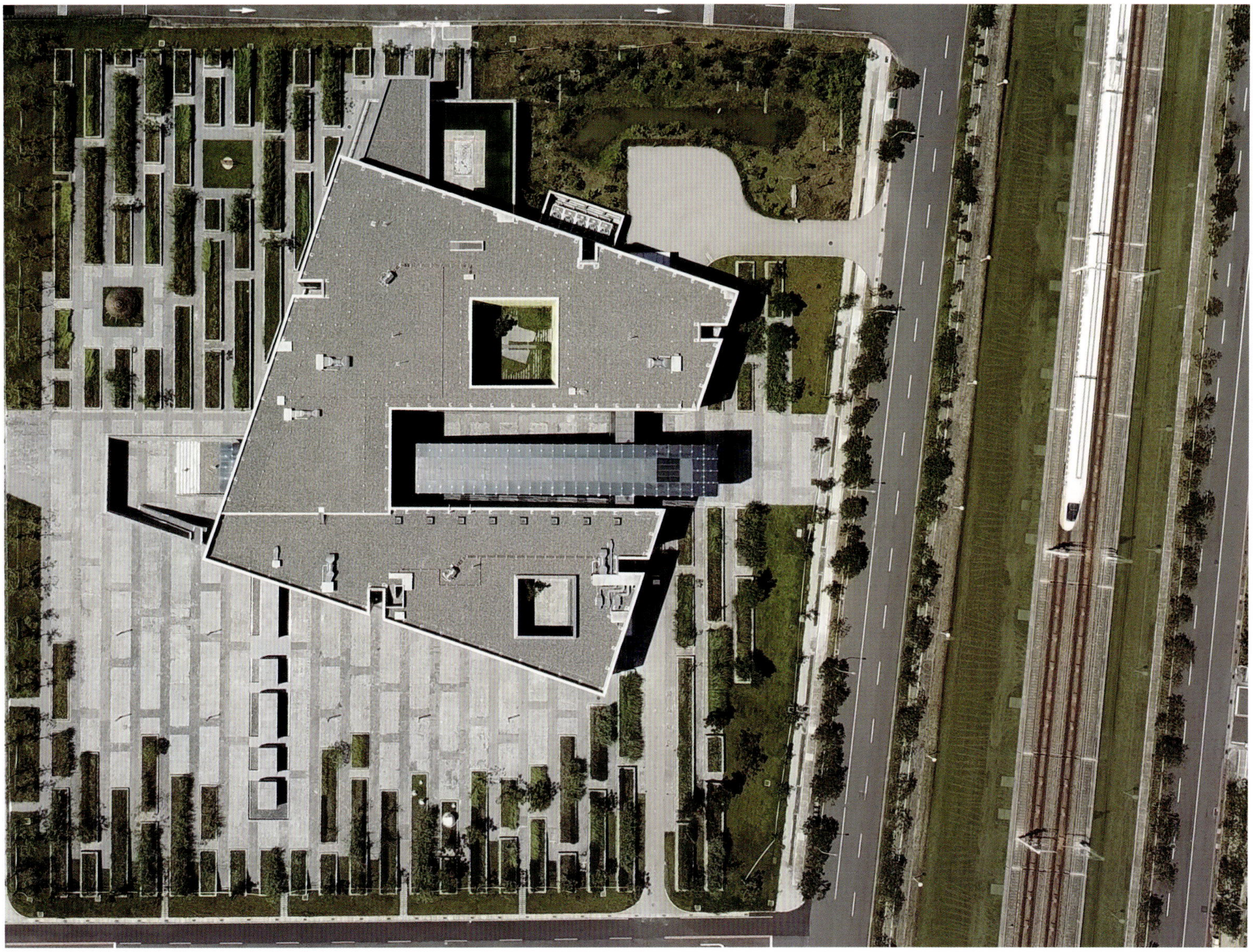

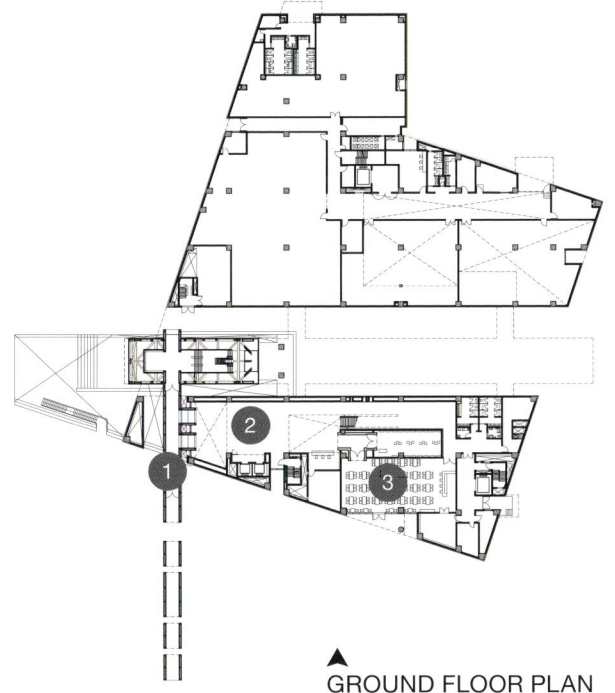

▲ GROUND FLOOR PLAN

1 Entrance
2 Lobby
3 Cafe

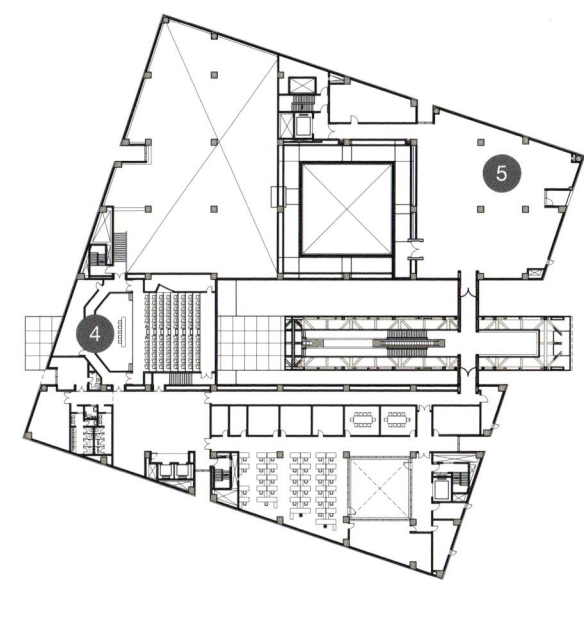

▲ 4TH FLOOR PLAN

4 Conference hall
5 Exhibition

From the entrance plaza, an enclosed metal walkway—split in four places to admit natural light—acts as a dramatic vestibule for the museum. The approach leads immediately to the tilted glass tunnel, which slices diagonally through the block, bringing visitors right up to the top of the building. While progressing through this passageway, visitors get the sense of traveling through the layers of archaeological dig, passing walls decorated with reliefs of human and animal figures, building anticipation for the surprise that awaits them at the top—a visual highlight in the form of high-speed trains that whisk by every few minutes.

From this glimpse of the modern world, visitors continue on to a winding ramp—again, within a tunnel—that descends in a counterclockwise direction to displays of prehistoric artifacts and traces of human activities. The route is punctuated by a courtyard with vibrant yellow walls that frames the sky as a perfect square. The direction of descent was intentionally designed to create the sense of winding back the clock, or traveling back in time, as if accompanying archaeologists as they dig through layers of history and make their discoveries. Visitors slowly make their way down one gentle slope, only to find another waiting at the next turn, creating the illusion of an expedition descending ever deeper into the archaeological realm. The changing orientation enhances the rise and fall of the slope, creating the perception of a never-ending pathway, when in reality, the journey spans just four floors.

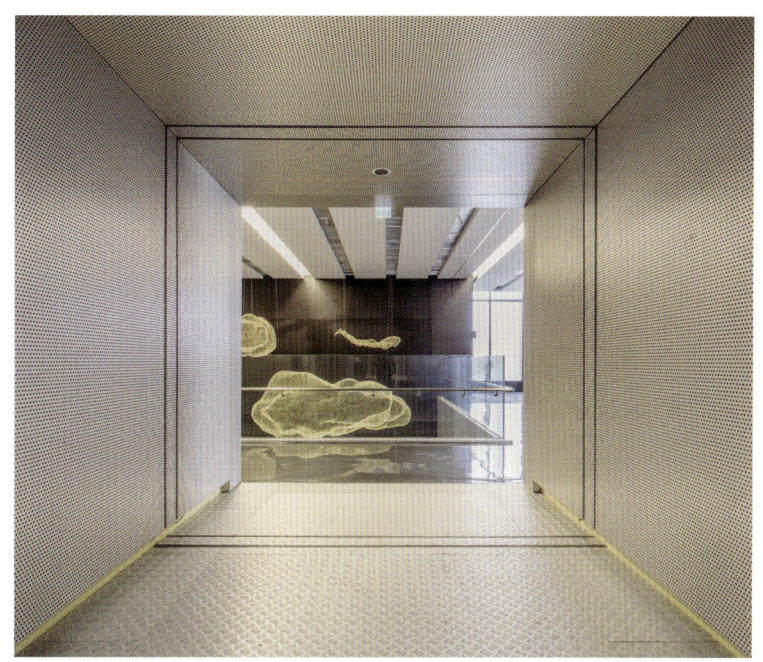

At the entrance to the museum, terraces bordered by river rocks evoke the retaining walls traditionally used in the rice fields of the region. This establishes an appropriate transition as visitors progress toward the building itself, its interlocking structures symbolizing the use of modern methods to carry out an archeological exploration.

Glimpses of the high-speed train, lasting no more than three seconds a time, provide the visual highlight at the end of the glass passageway, where the site's close proximity to the high-speed rail track allows visitors a close-up view from an observation deck. This silent, recurring scene is like a work of art in itself—and a powerful contrast to the static yet buzzing atmosphere of the exhibition spaces to come.

WUZHEN THEATER

Completed year: 2013 | Location: Zhejiang, China

Client: Wuzhen Tourism Co., Ltd.
Area: 22,500 m²

After the ravages of time and a devastating fire in 1999, the historic water town of Wuzhen was meticulously restored. To enhance its appeal, the developer wanted a theater that would provide world-class facilities without overwhelming the town's historic buildings. To meet this brief, KYA designed two performance spaces as interlocking ovals, inspired by the rare and auspicious "twin lotus." The theater's rounded forms and canted walls, made using bricks and wood—building materials that have been used in Wuzhen for thousands of years—allow this impressive modern build to nestle comfortably among its ancient neighbors.

The main auditorium has a wrap-around foyer that receives light through a glazed facade, covered by a "broken-ice" screen of reclaimed wood, zigzagging like the leaves of a fan. The wood was sourced from old boats that once navigated Wuzhen's rivers—a show of respect to the town's historic mode of transportation. Light spills through this screen and onto the white marble floors within, casting a series of intricate shadows that contrast with the simplicity of the interior.

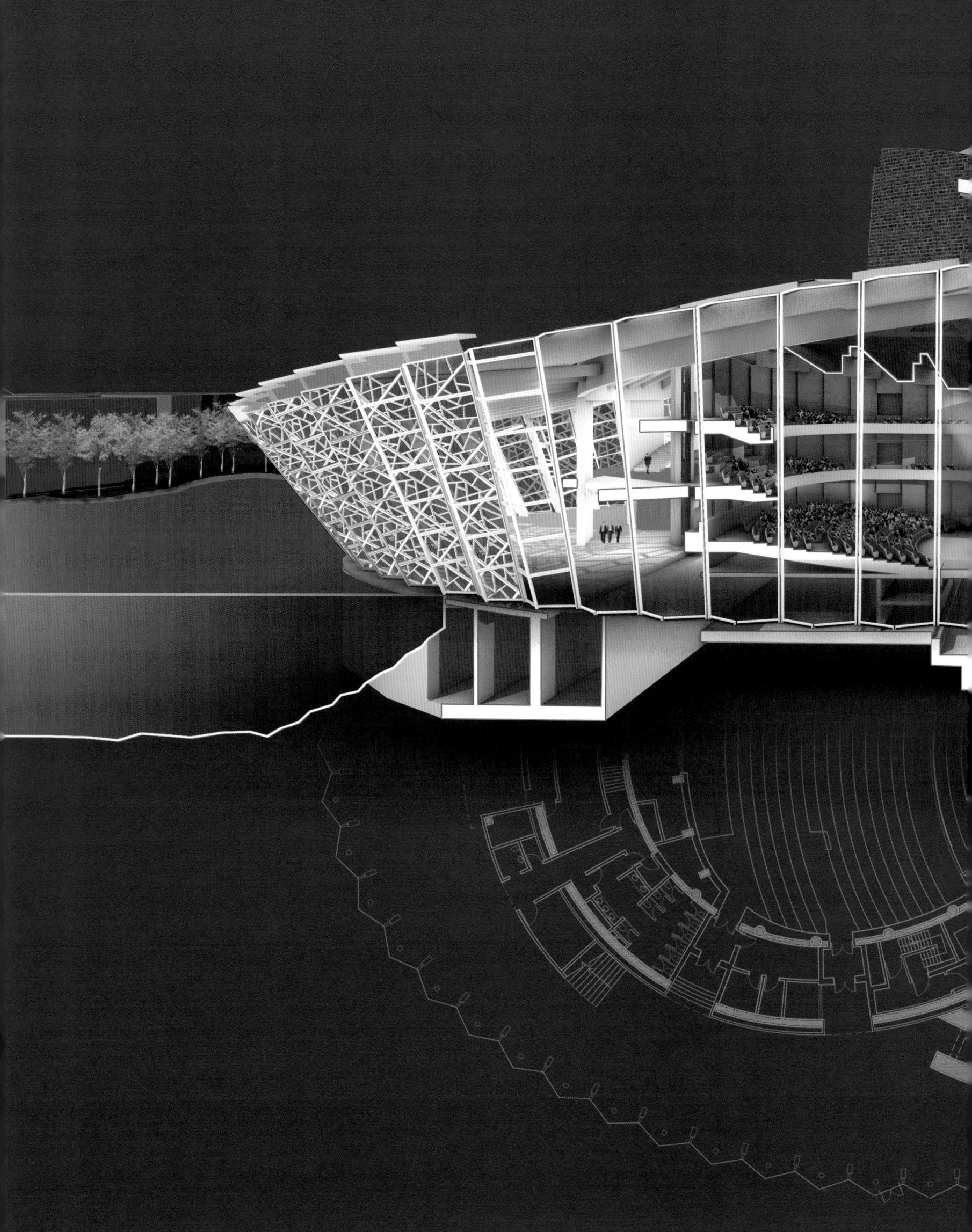

Sectional perspective through the two performing spaces.

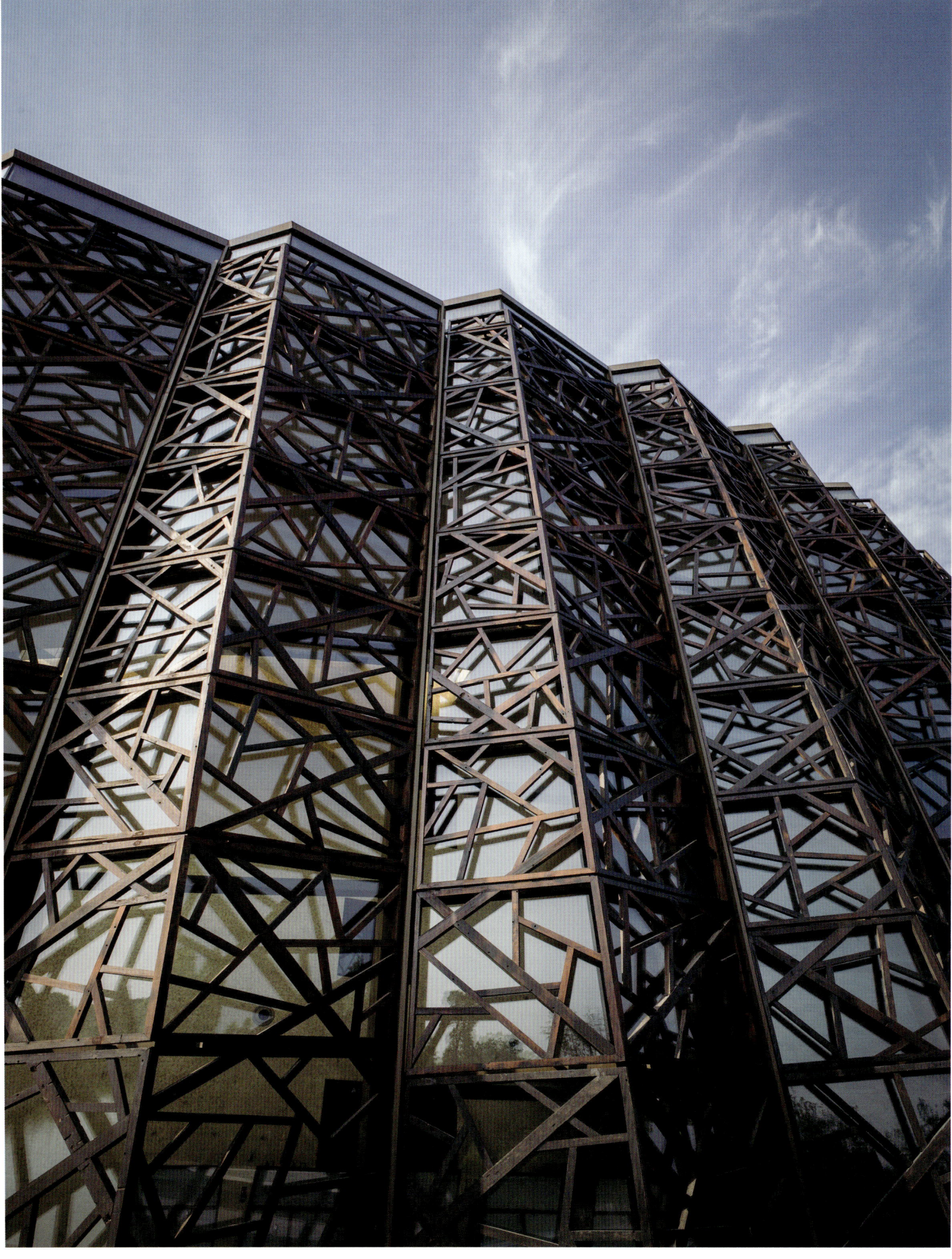

Thick petal-like wall segments, clad in ancient supersized brick, enclose the foyer of the smaller auditorium. The bricks were hand-stacked in arcs to form each segment, each layered over the next to form an ellipse of twenty-two overlapping walls. This alternation of transparent and opaque dematerializes the mass of the theater, which now stands as a symbolic bridge between Wuzhen's old quarter and the newer parts of town.

◀
Walls of gold leaf enclose the 1200-seat auditorium, in which the interior is lined with a patterned repoussé.

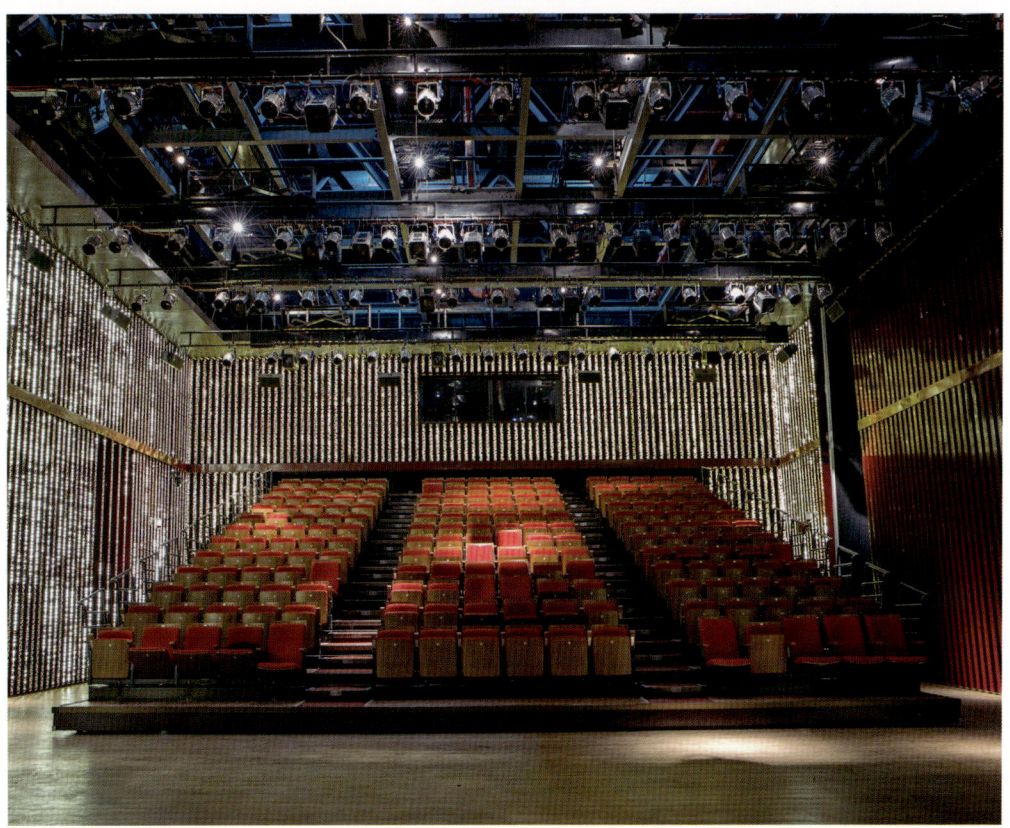

▶ Walls of silver wrap up the 600-seat auditorium, in which the interior is lined in a gold mesh.

Wuzhen has long been famous for its blue calico—an indigo-dyed cloth that features contrasting white floral motifs. As a tribute to this traditional craft, contemporary interpretations of these motifs were used to adorn the ceiling and walls of the main auditorium.

The theater as a whole presents itself as a modern, high-tech performance venue, yet its close association with the local culture gives it an identity that sets it apart from other venues of its kind, both Eastern and Western. This is a project that the locals speak of proudly, richly deserving its acclaim as "the most beautiful theater in China."

WATER-MOON MONASTERY

Completed year: 2012 | Location: Taipei, Taiwan

Client: Dharma Drum Mountain Nung Chan Monastery
Area: 8,056 m²

The Water-Moon Monastery is a work of religious architecture that sits quietly facing the Keelung River, with Mount Datun as its backdrop. Past two walls between the busy highway and the supernatural space, the view immediately opens up to an 80-meter-long lotus pond which reflects parts of the shrine at the far end—a mirage of the oversized colonnades and the flowing golden drapes in between—appearing and disappearing with the ripples. This dual image invites visitors to sit on the steps around the pond and contemplate this juxtaposition of reality and illusion. One may ponder on a Zen question, "is it the wind? Is it the drapes? Or is it the unsettling mind that's causing the movement?"

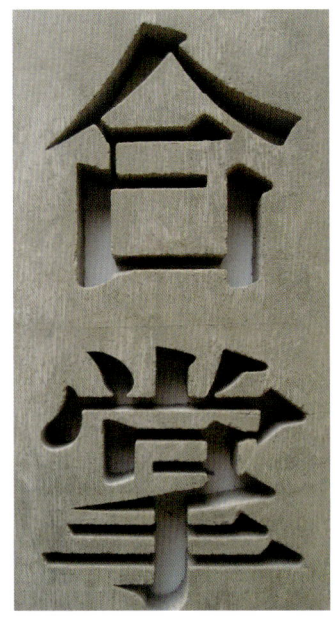
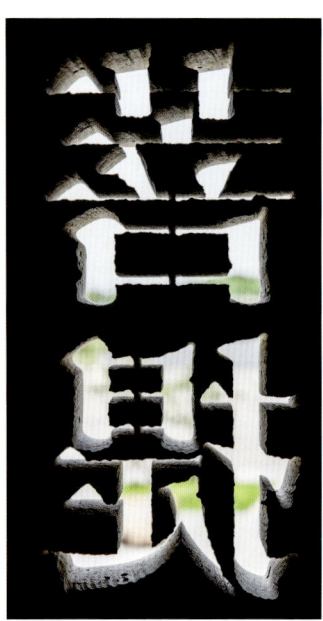

The exterior wall of the building adjacent to the main hall features the 5,180-word Diamond Sutra, engraved in large Chinese characters. Each precast concrete panel was perforated with a single character—reflecting the Chinese movable type invented centuries ago to reproduce this and other scriptures, while also cleverly balancing the primitive and the modern by employing contemporary fabrication techniques to present an ancient text.

As daylight shines through these apertures, the Buddha's teachings are brought to life in the interior spaces, projected as a text of light, and after rain, the text is seen reflected on the still-wet exterior pavements. This unique presentation of the sutra was designed to complement the design of the monastery and, combined with the tranquility of the setting, to silently communicate the philosophy that underpins it.

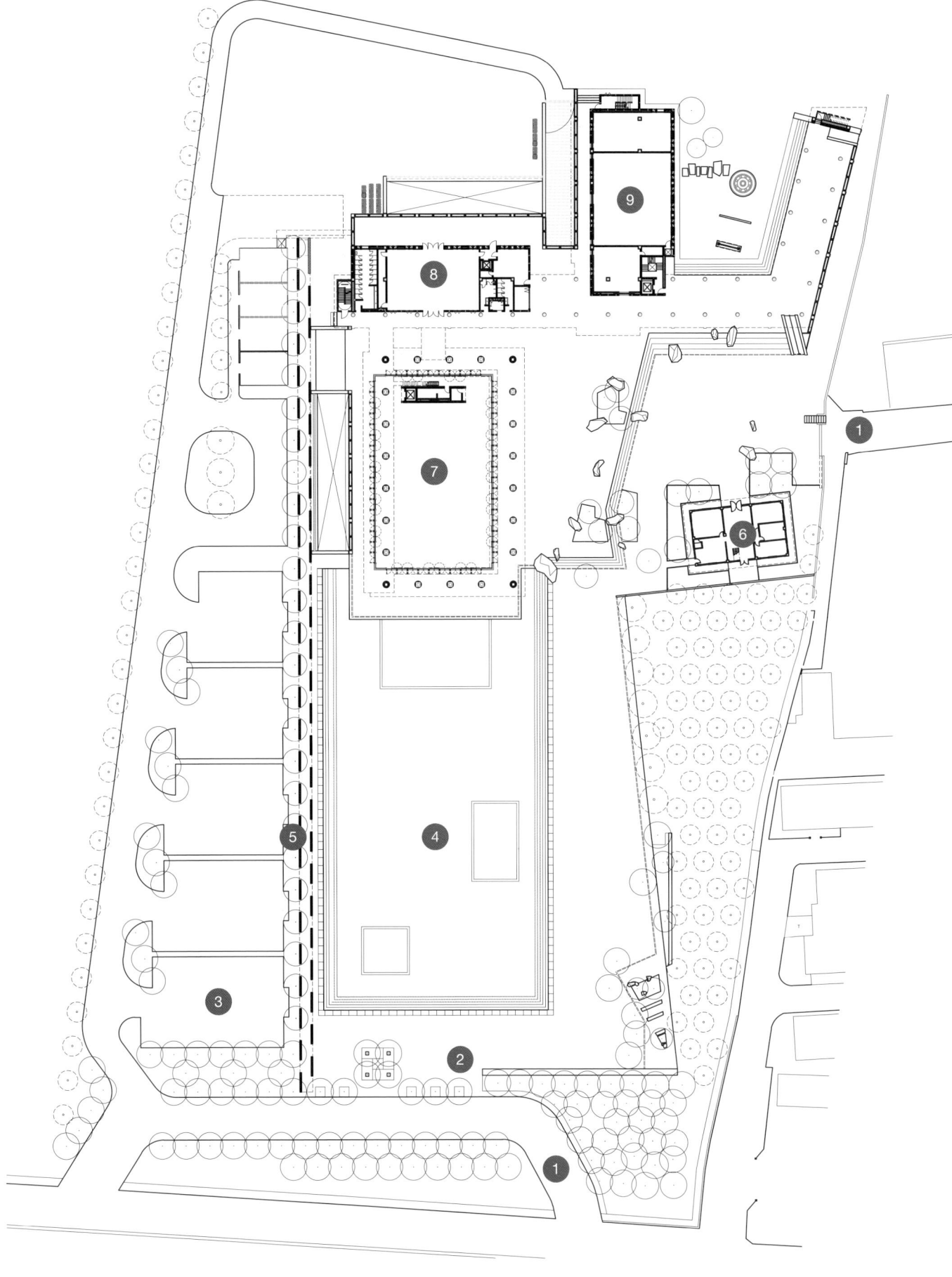

GROUND FLOOR PLAN

1 Entrance
2 Spirit screen
3 Outdoor parking
4 Lotus pond
5 Pilgrimage passage
6 Historic building
7 Main hall
8 Dining hall
9 Lecture hall

Between the main hall and the stone wall is a large open courtyard that appears untouched by time, populated by a series of gigantic rocks that rest comfortably in place, holding their ground as if they were installed long ago. As Michael Speaks, Dean of Syracuse University's School of Architecture, puts it, these irregularly sited boulders "recall another era, if not another age. One is left to wonder whether the architect placed these massive rocks in the courtyard, or whether the courtyard was designed around them to accommodate their glacial, rather than human, placement" (Speaks 1). Such are the questions that tend to arise when one enters this space, but they are usually left unresolved—and that, in itself, is part of the fascination of the place.

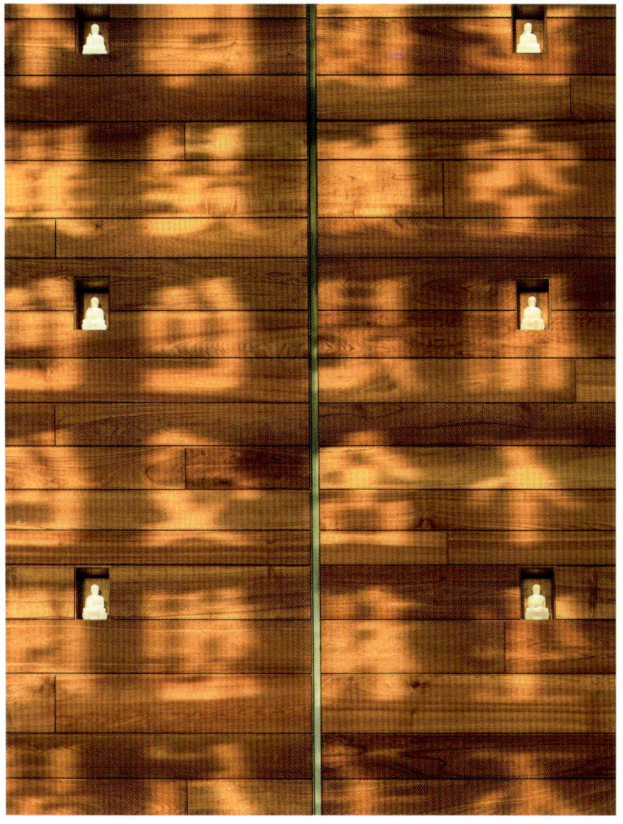

Suspended on top of a transparent glass base, the wooden exterior of the main hall appears to float in midair. Employing the same technique as the "Diamond Sutra," here the characters of the "Heart Sutra" were punched through an expansive internal wall, revealing their meaning as daylight projects them onto hard surfaces. As the sun moves across the sky, these sacred words of light dance across concrete walls and columns, mirroring the effect of a prayer wheel, and seemingly slowing the passage of time itself.

To the left of the vast pond, a 550-meter-long walkway is sandwiched between two concrete walls. This not only provides a circulation route where visitors may stumble upon worshipers and nuns, but also constitutes what Speaks (2015) describes as:

> A wondrous sensory mixing chamber, where the controlled stream of noise and chaos from the city is reconditioned and made to blend with the sound of prayers, visitors' chatter, and the soft shuffle of those moving about on concrete floors. (p. 1)

Daylight composes a steady rhythm of light and shade across the hallway, too, offering a metaphor for the recurring ups and downs of the human experience. The powerful aura of this space can soothe a troubled visitor, encouraging him to embrace life in both dark times and light.

WATER-MOON MONASTERY

The primary material used for the monastery was concrete, its unadorned facade and muted color scheme intended to reflect the simplicity of Zen Buddhism. Inside the main hall, 108 Buddha sculptures are recessed into the wooden north-facing wall. Opposite this, a large glass wall allows natural light in and provides a broad view of the sky—at certain times of day, reflections of the sculptures appear in the sky, as if sitting among the clouds.

Whether you're a devoted Buddhist looking for a place of worship, or a secular traveler seeking a refuge from the world, Water-Moon Monastery is the perfect place to focus on mind and spirit. The stresses of the city are left behind, and a journey through this serene space leaves visitors in a profoundly more relaxed state than when they arrived. With its unique presentation of Buddhist scriptures, together with an overall design that embodies Zen teachings, it offers an enlightening space for all.

CITATION
Speaks, Michael. "Quickening and Slowing: The Genius of Kris Yao's Singular Modernism." *30 x 30 Kris Yao / Artech Selected Works*", edited by Kris Yao. Beijing, 2015.

FENG ZIKAI ARTS CENTER

Design year: 2020 | Location: Tongxiang, China

FENG ZIKAI ARTS CENTER

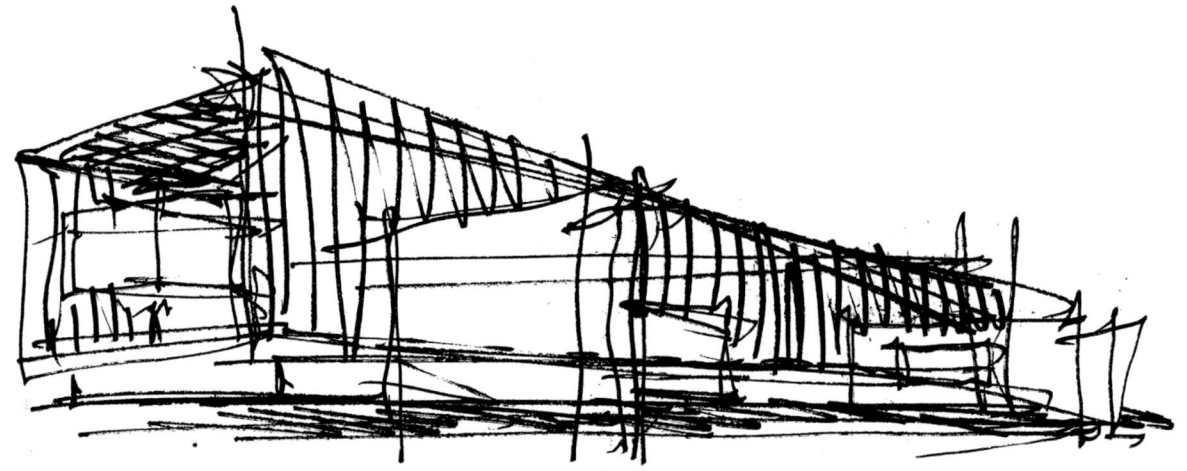

Client: Tongxiang Zhendong New District Construction Investment Co., Ltd.
Area: 110,059 m²

The arts center established in honor of the 20th-century painter and scholar Feng Zikai is located in the great artist's birthplace—the city of Tongxiang, in China's Zhejiang province, which houses a dense river network and beautiful natural surroundings. Tongxiang is a typical Jiangnan water town with a long history and a profound cultural heritage. It has nurtured a number of modern intellectuals, including Feng Zikai and Mao Dun, and it hosts a handful of cultural events each year—the Wuzhen Theater Festival, the Zikai Cup Chinese Comics Exhibition, and the Mao Dun Literary Award, to name just a few.

This building group centers on a long, rectangular museum. To the east stands the "moon-lit" concert hall, and to the west, the "sun-lit" performance spaces. The three components form a U-shaped plan around the Sun-Moon Pond, where the music and theater centers gaze at one another across the water. To the north, 21 rectangular stone pillars form a colonnade that divides the entrance courtyard into an array of boulevards, and frames views out to the beautiful Phoenix Lake beyond. A pedestrian walkway cuts through the boulevard and the man-made pond, straight toward the art museum, which is designed like an oversized square tube, containing multiple floating boxes of gallery spaces.

Feng Zikai was well known for combining Western painting styles with traditional Chinese techniques. Borrowing from this, the facade of the art center closely resembles a pattern found on traditional window lattices, yet the construction and delivery of the cladding uses the latest technology. And jumping between vernacular bricks and modern oxidized aluminum panels, the facade reinterprets local Jiangnan architecture with a language belonging to the present day. The resulting motifs cast striking shadows onto the walls and floors within, injecting life and playfulness into the communal areas of this conventionally classy art venue. The center reflects Feng Zikai's enduring love for his hometown, while also mirroring the essence of his artistic achievements through its design language.

▶
Feng Zikai was a pioneering cartoonist and an influential painter, scholar, and educator.

▲
The layout consists of a tube-like museum, the "moon-lit" concert hall, and the "sun-lit" performance spaces.

▶ The Feng Zikai Arts Center reinterprets vernacular architectural elements with a façade pattern closely resembling that of a traditional window lattice.

HEFEI CENTRAL LIBRARY

Completed year: 2023　|　Location: Hefei, China

104 HEFEI CENTRAL LIBRARY

Client: HeFei Municipal Administration of Culture and Tourism
Area: 65,790 m²

Hefei Central Library is part of a cultural complex located in an extended arts zone and sports park bordering the north shore of Swan Lake, in the city of Hefei. Housed underground are a parking garage, subway station, and ancillary commercial facilities, while above ground the complex consists of three elements—the library, an automated storage-and-retrieval system, and the City Exhibition Hall (designed to host meetings and exhibitions). The hall takes the form of a long rectangular block, 33 meters high, and the library sits adjacent to this, a 63-meter-high square block. The rectilinear forms of both play off the rounded mass of the Hefei Grand Theater sited across the water, and both rise from a podium that forms a plaza to the front, and gives elevated views over the lake and central business district to the rear.

Broad stairs lead up to the plaza, both providing access and a place to congregate, sit quietly, or watch outdoor performances. Further pedestrian routes then form a continuous link between the two buildings, leading through to the waterfront side of the complex.

As with so many of KYA's public commissions, the goal was to reinforce a sense of community by offering residents a place to pause, contemplate the beauty of the landscape, and seek enlightenment within. The axiality of the plaza contrasts with the undulating shoreline and the forest of high-rises in the city beyond. The building masses are also softened by the presence of trees and water, making this versatile complex a retreat from the density and frenzied pace of the metropolis.

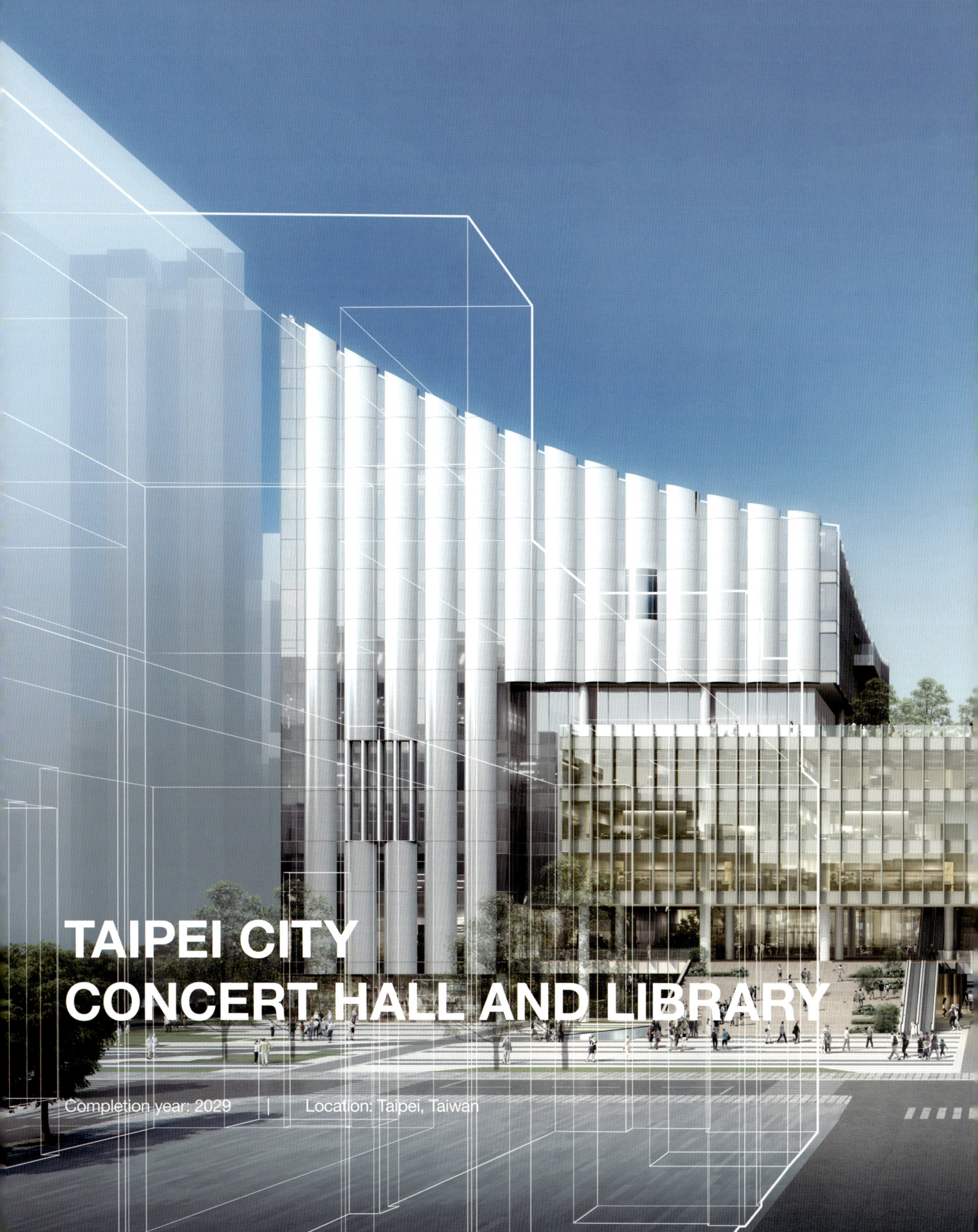

TAIPEI CITY CONCERT HALL AND LIBRARY

Client: Taipei City Government, Public Works Department, Hydraulic Engineering Office
Area: 87,745 m²

The unusual location of the Taipei City Concert Hall and Library will set it apart from other performance venues in the city. Spanning four blocks defined and bordered by intersecting alleys, this new landmark hopes to recall the city at street scale, where narrow lanes between low-rise buildings characterize the majority of the metropolis. The project is located in the East District, which is populated with countless cafés and independent stores, and will flow into the ground-level retail spaces upon completion. By scaling the complex back to a more human level, KYA aims to create a unique music center and library "amid the streets," cleverly integrated with its diverse surroundings and capable of satisfying the demand for both formal and informal cultural events.

The roof takes the form of two concave arcs, which on one hand reduce the large mass of the building, and on the other, form a distinct silhouette that will be recognizable from a distance. The design of the facade was inspired by the ancient bamboo slips once used for writing documents, and the simple lines of the Western musical stave; it has great simplicity, yet it encompasses spaces of great complexity.

There are three formal performance venues: a 1,500-seat symphony hall, a 600-seat multimedia space, and a 500-seat conference center, each contained in a light box. When night falls, these boxes will radiate a gentle, warm light, casting a romantic glow over the neighboring streets.

The new cultural convention will have two main components: a library to the north, and a music center to the south. The former is intended to be "a library of the future"—no longer simply a place to read and borrow books, but rather a space in which people can gather to exchange knowledge and ideas. It will become an "information exchange," or a "shared communication lounge," where people can read, meet, and cultivate their minds.

Likewise, the music center is intended to be a concert hall for the people, able to cater for professional performances, yet flexible enough to allow for more impromptu events. The technical equipment in the 1,500-seat symphony hall will meet the highest international standards, allowing the hall to compete

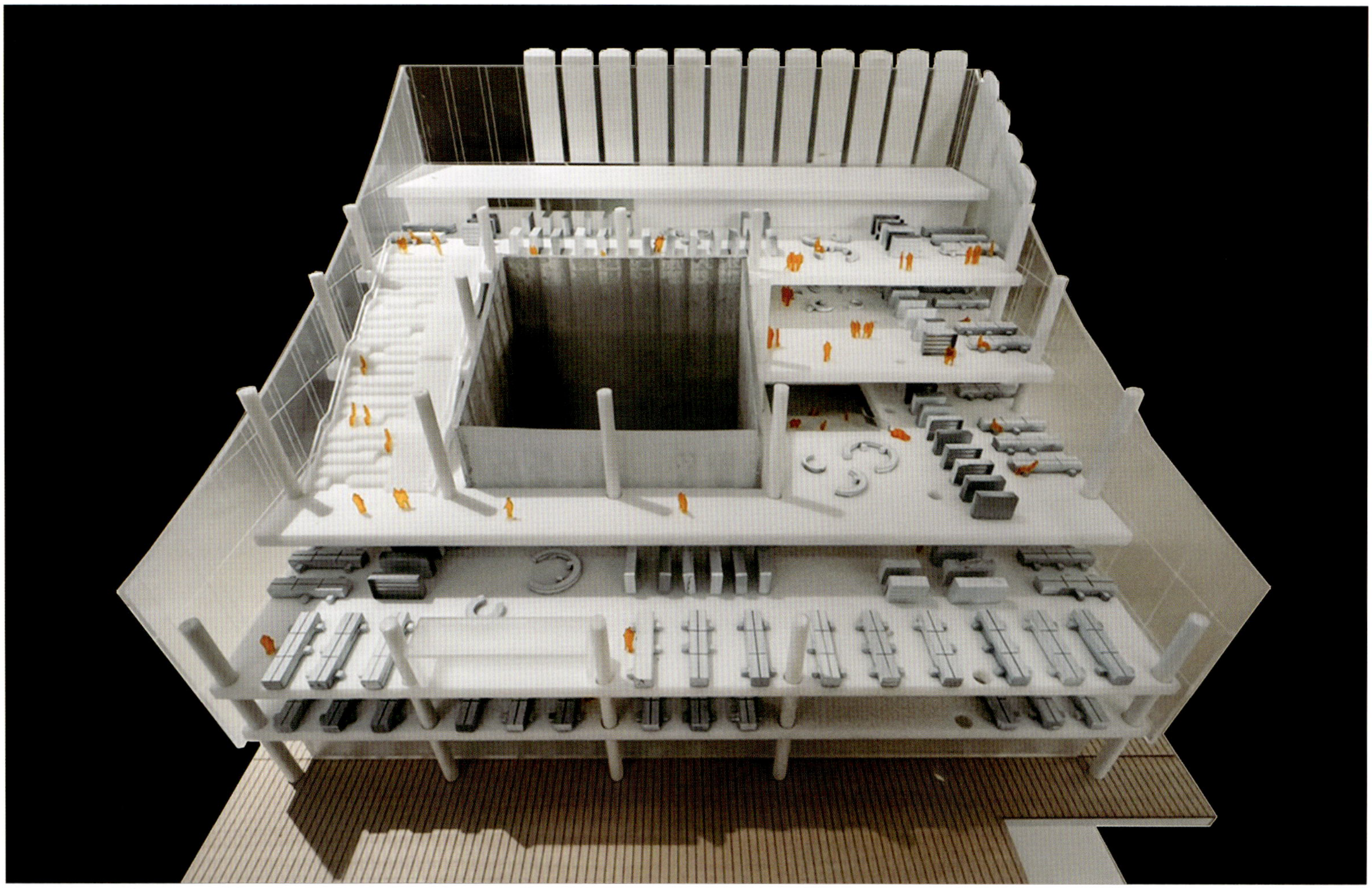

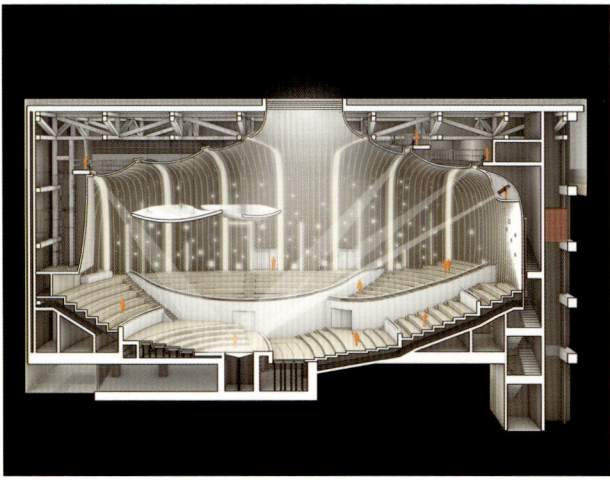

with the best music venues in the world. Pockets of free space here and there will then overturn the traditional divide between performer and audience, providing visitors with places where they will be free to watch, perform, or otherwise participate as they please. In the same spirit, the complex will free up numerous urban rest-stops throughout for public use, including the front plaza, green belts, and the broad steps leading up to the entrance, as well as the elevated platform, shared lobby, and roof garden.

With its variety of spatial depths, elegance of architectural forms, and wealth of programs, the Taipei City Concert Hall and Library will become a new cultural landmark, fully aware of the community it serves and the symbol it bears. Together, we patiently await its completion.

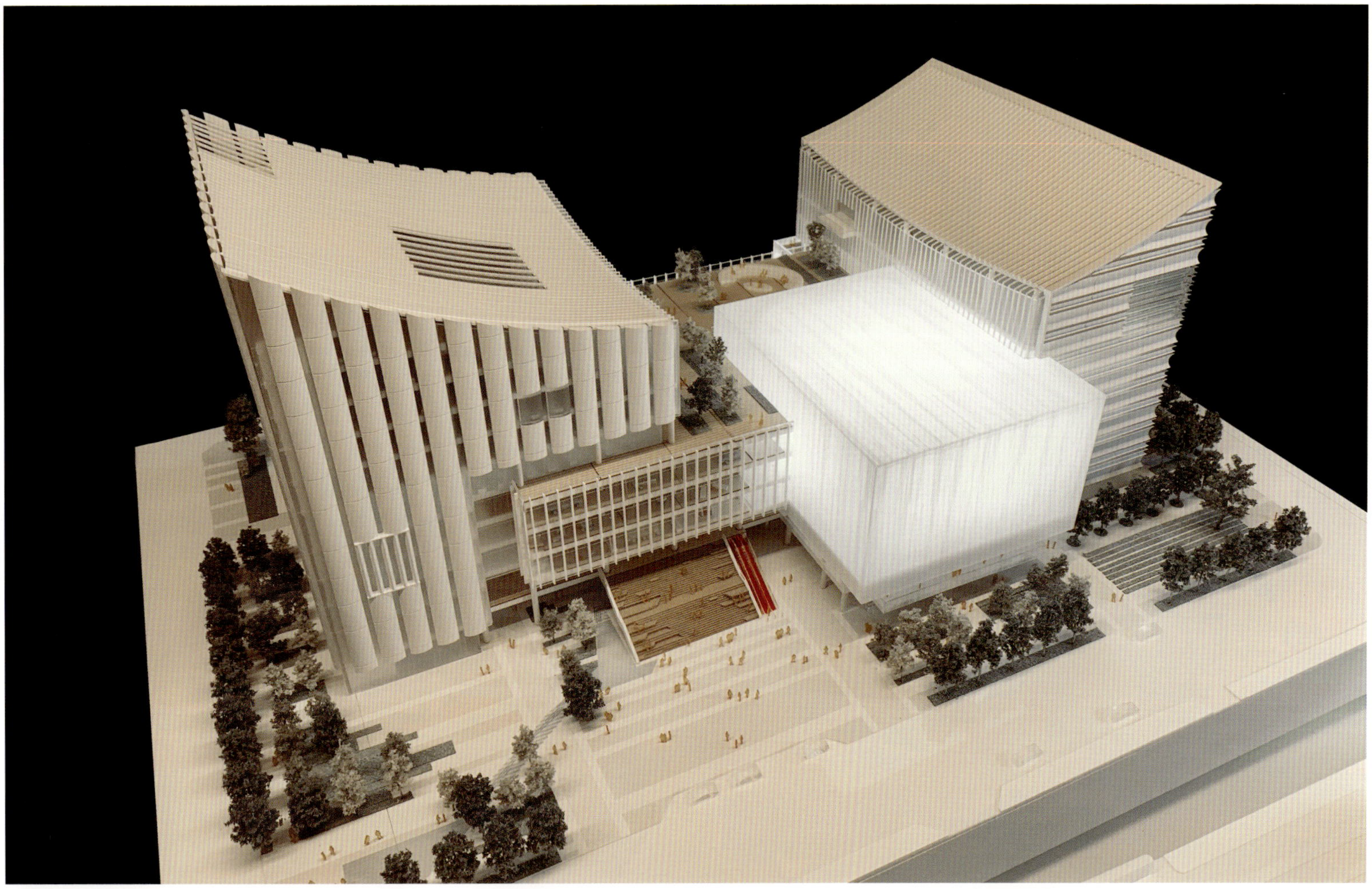

▲
A study model of facade patterns.

▶
A sectional model showing spatial relations between the conference center, the library atrium, and the reading spaces.

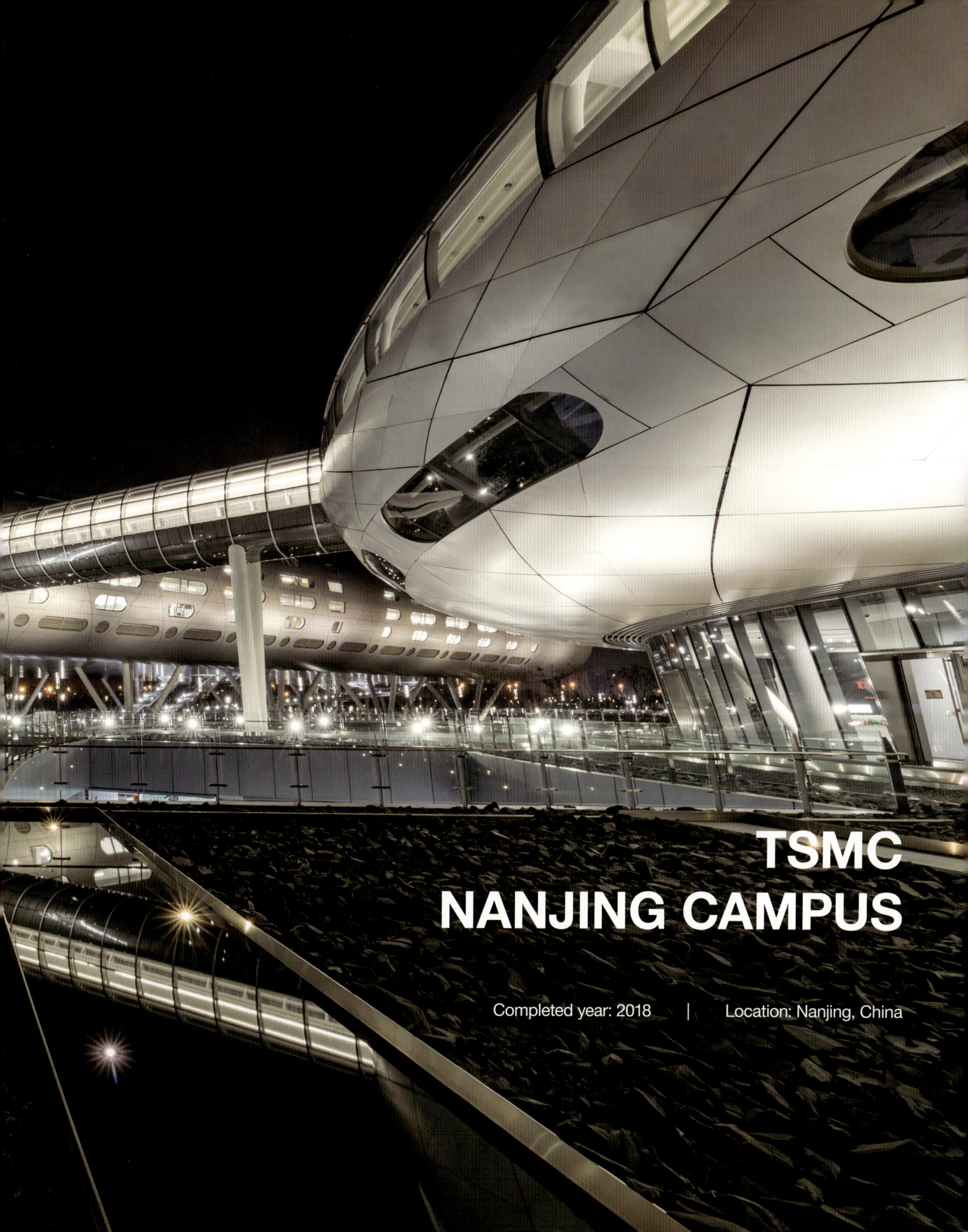

TSMC NANJING CAMPUS

Completed year: 2018 | Location: Nanjing, China

Client: Taiwan Semiconductor Manufacturing Company, Ltd. (TSMC)

The completion of the TSMC Nanjing Campus achieves a significant milestone in the establishment of high-tech enterprises in China. This futuristic complex, set amid lush vegetation, brings production and administration work together on the same campus, in an environment that maximizes productivity and also ensures the well-being of its workforce.

KYA conceived this complex as though it were a single building, linking the component parts and allowing them to expand outward like ripples in a pond. In the R&D tube, the circulation of office workers and products are integrated, and a green skywalk will link the first phase of office development to the second. The spaces are designed to encourage communication between employees, and to create diversity and interest. The horizontal layout of office spaces is designed to promote a highly efficient workflow, while landscaping and skylights provide a pleasant working environment, full of greenery and bathed in natural light. The goal is a 21st-century factory office, with an integrated approach to sustainability, technology, and user comfort.

The plan consists of two cylindrical semiconductor fabrication plants ("fabs"), placed in two opposite corners of the site. An 850-meter-long tubular R&D office then runs between them on a diagonal, with a large lake at one end, while an entry rotunda strictly controls access into the chip giant's den. However, the first phase of the project only saw the completion of the entrance building, the lake, the fab adjacent to the lake, and two-thirds of the R&D tube.

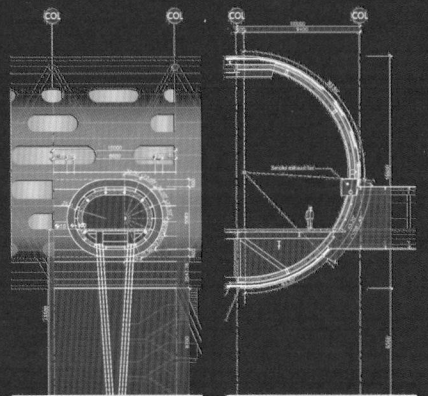
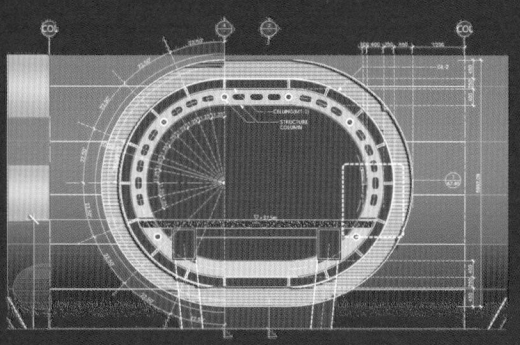

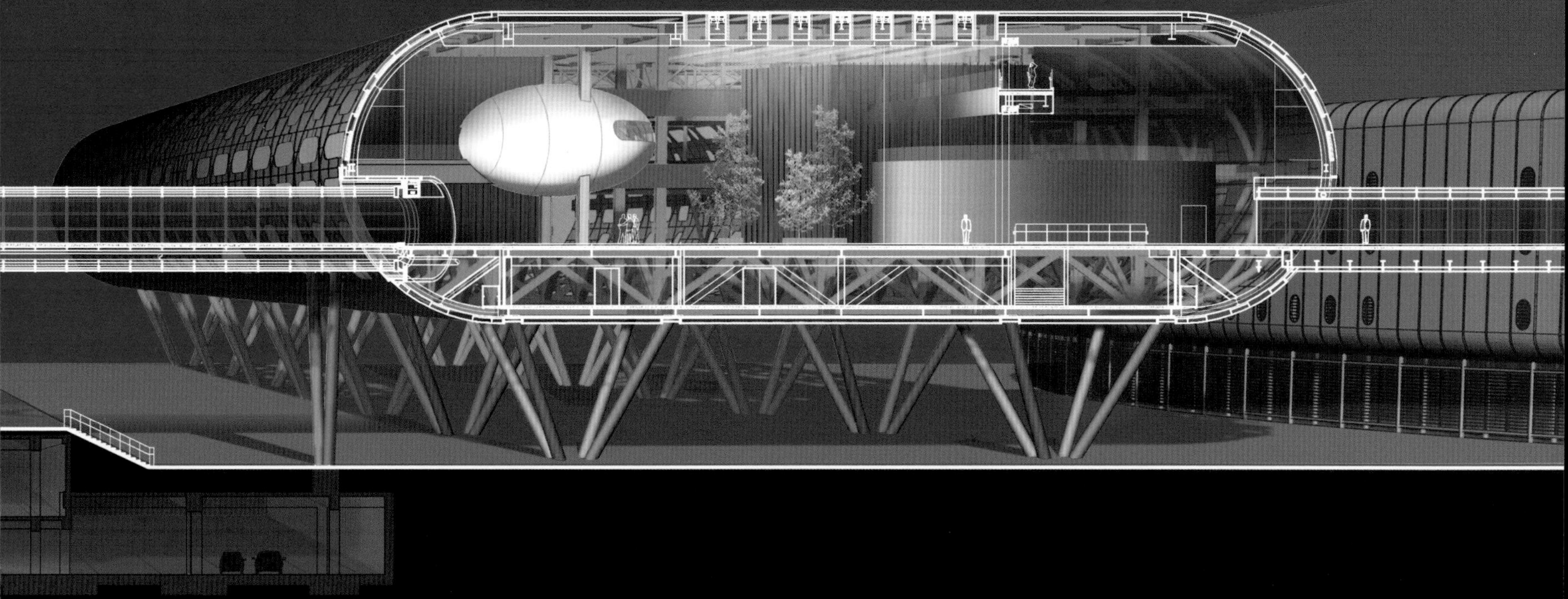

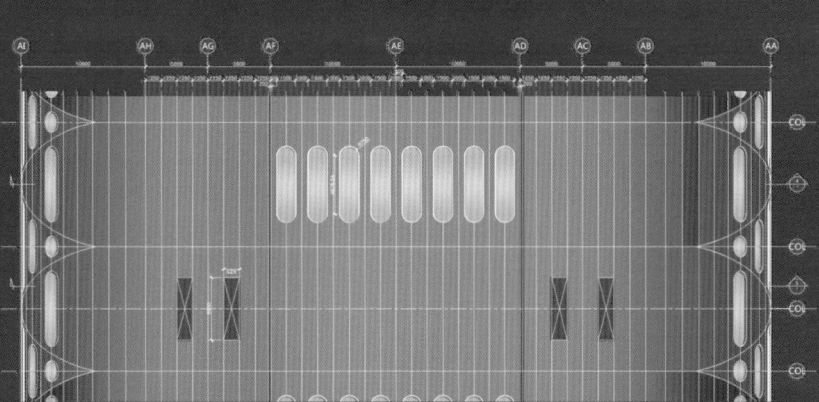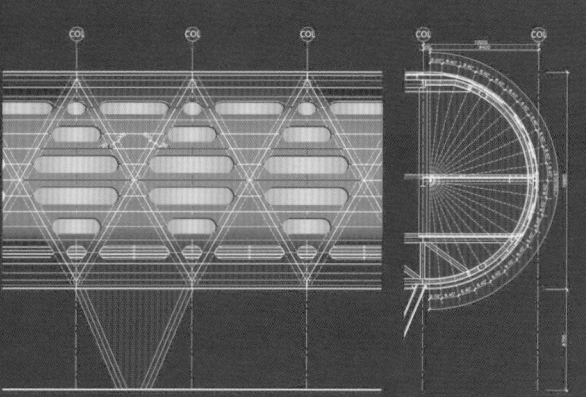

Sectional perspective through office spaces and corridors.

▶

The interior of the R&D tube appears to belong to another space and time—creating the sense of a science-fiction movie set, or an oversized spacecraft on a voyage of discovery. The colors and textures of the materials, the peculiar shape of the skylights, and the unorthodox floating compartments all speak the language of high technology.

Facing a site with an area 100 times larger than is typical for most architectural projects, KYA decided to incorporate a great number of green spaces as one of its primary design concepts. The team envisioned the campus as "a fab in the forest," with lush greenery surrounding an innovative and human-friendly workplace. The architectural design centers around circular volumes, referencing TSMC's prominent role in wafer fabrication as one of the leading semiconductor manufacturers in the world. The tubular R&D office, the control center, and the fab plants all take on a variation of the disk structure, each with a gray and white metal cladding, and each hovering in its own space above the forest.

The lake, which stretches 180 meters in diameter, provides scenic views and enhances biodiversity by mitigating the microclimate and absorbing excess water after heavy rains. The elevated buildings also leave a generous portion of land free for existing vegetation to spread, increasing the integration of indoors and outdoors in the future.

In an enterprise of this kind, spontaneous exchanges between individuals and between different departments are crucial to fostering morale and sparking innovation. By extending the buildings into the forest and freeing up the ground plane, employees will be encouraged to exercise and socialize around the campus. This could almost be the model for a colony on Mars, but with an easy flow of work and relaxation from indoors to outdoors, and absolutely no need for protective gear.

HAINAN ENERGY TRADING BUILDING

Completed year: 2022 | Location: Haikou, China

HAINAN ENERGY TRADING BUILDING

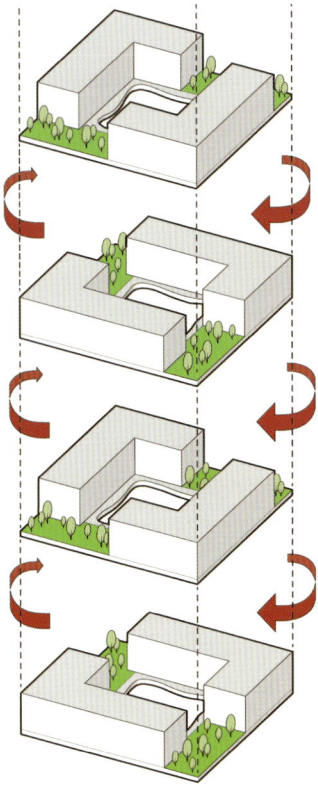

Client: Hainan Intelligent Center Development Co., Ltd.
Area: 65,726 m²

The Hainan Energy Trading Building stands proudly in Jiangdong New District, an emerging industrial, financial, and residential development on the outskirts of Haikou, capital of China's Hainan province. The Yankuang Group, owner and occupier of the building, specializes in mining production and sales, high-end coal processing, and modern logistics, and the early entry of the firm's headquarters in Jiangdong New District paves the way for other leading business to follow suit. The building is a floating box above a landscaped ground floor, and an impressive central courtyard greets visitors as they enter the atrium. The rigid lines of the exterior contrast with the sky gardens positioned at regular intervals—a blend of rigidity and softness that creates a harmonious whole, mirroring the fledgling district's aim of combining existing site conditions with cutting-edge technology.

The sustainable design of this project goes hand-in-hand with Yankuang Group's green-energy initiatives. Firstly, greenery is maximized with the exterior sky gardens as well as abundant planting in the interior. The sky gardens punch in opposing corners in an orderly fashion, occurring every four floors and rotating 90 degrees each time. Inside, multiple tiers of curving balconies span the spaces between the elevator boxes and these are densely packed with unruly plants that spill out over their edges. This is a nature-filled space, designed to provide employees with a sense of peace and well-being.

Secondly, the courtyard creates a pleasant microclimate, made possible by an effective shading and stack ventilation strategies in the 75-meter-high atrium. Due to the differences in air pressure, temperature, and density levels at each floor, incoming fresh air forces stale air upward and out through the roof opening, keeping the interior well ventilated and thermally comfortable for its users.

▲
Top view of the atrium.

▶
TYPICAL LOW ZONE
FLOOR PLAN
1 Office
2 Atrium
3 Sky garden

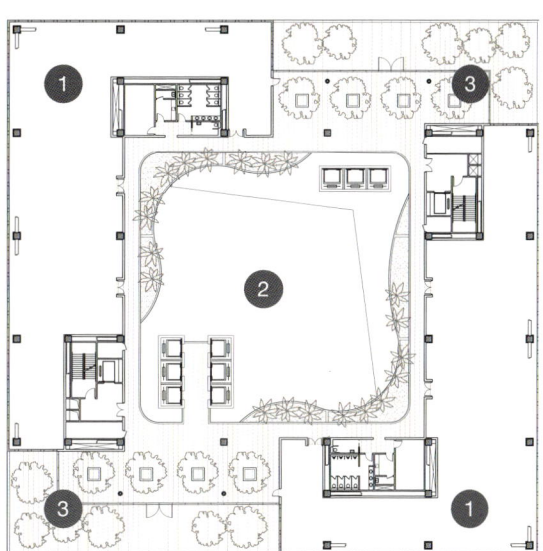
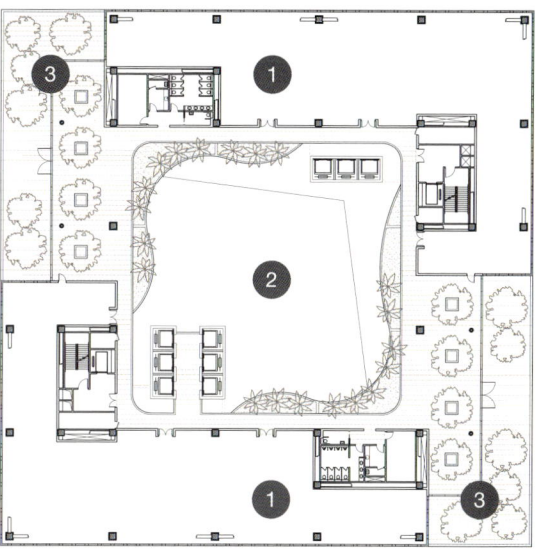

Sectional perspective showing the central atrium, the sky gardens, and the mega-bracing.

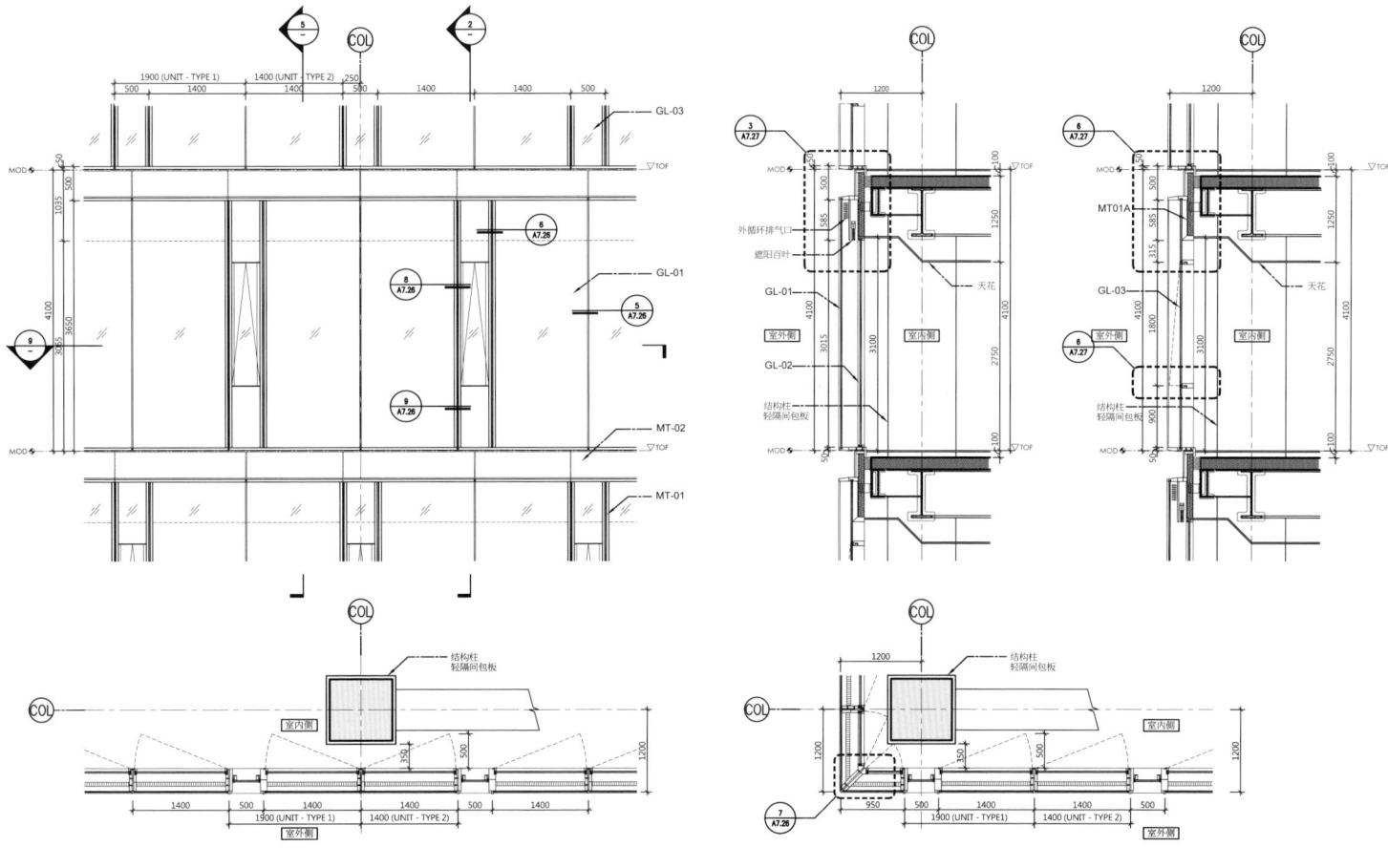

▲ ▶
FAÇADE DETAIL

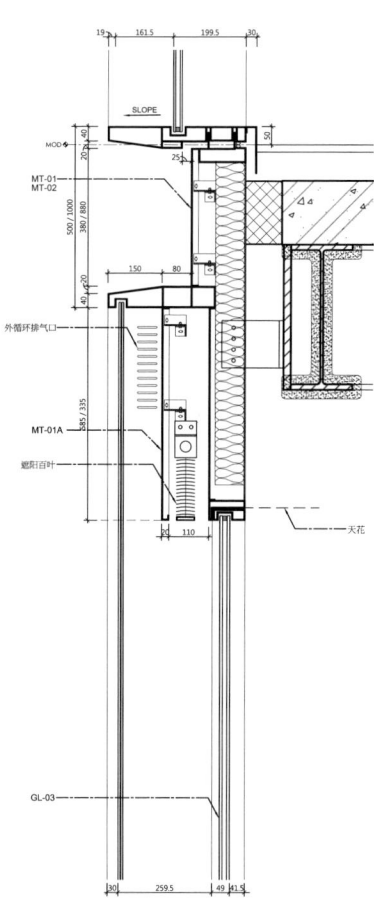

One particularly spectacular feature is the energy-efficient double skin façade design with high-transparent glass, which from the inside provides office workers with unobstructed views of the coast and downtown area, and from the outside proudly showcases the building's structure—clean, slender, yet very robust. None of the pillars interrupts the spacious sky gardens that rotate every four levels, allowing the volume of the other four floors above to cantilever up to 14 meters. This is achieved through mega-bracings that minimize the lateral deflection of the structure, and provide a feasible solution for strengthening earthquake resistance.

Sufficient daylight pours through the double skin facade on all four sides, lowering the need for artificial lighting. The electric louvers between the inner and outer glass layers can be automatically adjusted by the sensors of the solar tracking system, which, together with the intelligent lighting control system, greatly increase the comfort of the indoor environment and reduce the use of air-conditioning system to reach energy-saving goals. In addition, the slanted roof and the offset facade at four-story intervals provide the sky gardens and the office spaces with ample natural light, while shading most of the corridors and atrium to prevent overheating in the warm Hainan climate. The roof also pays tribute to the traditional Jiangnan home, in which rain is designed to run down slanted planes on four sides and gather in a square courtyard below, signifying the flow and retention of good fortune into a family—or in this context, a company. These design strategies also greatly increase the sustainability of the building, making the Hainan Energy Trading Building a standout example in the world of green architecture.

▲ Horizontal view of the plant-filled balconies.

▶ View down the gorge-like atrium that performs microclimate adjustments.

FOXCONN HEADQUARTERS SHANGHAI

Completed year: 2019 | Location: Shanghai, China

148 FOXCONN HEADQUARTERS SHANGHAI

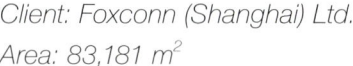

Client: Foxconn (Shanghai) Ltd.
Area: 83,181 m²

Lujiazui, Shanghai's glitzy financial district, is host to the city's architectural beauty pageant. Famously dominated by three of the world's tallest buildings—towers by SOM, KPF, and Gensler that locals refer to as the kitchen brush, the bottle opener, and the corkscrew—participants overlook the Huangpu River in order of height, with the shortest at the front, and the tallest at the back, all displaying themselves with great confidence. The headquarters of the Taiwanese manufacturer Foxconn stands modestly in the first row, yet it manages to retain its own sense of identity, with a meticulously crafted design that immediately sets it apart from the competition.

The building comprises a cluster of four slender towers, separated by recesses on either side, and the distinctive three-dimensional zigzag pattern of the glazing gives the facades an energy that is lacking in its more conventional neighbors. The facets of these diamond-like units break up and reconfigure the reflection of its surroundings, offering a unique view of the city and an appearance that shifts with the weather and the time of day. Embodying Foxconn's strong corporate identity, this is also an intelligent and sustainable building, providing a modern workspace characterized by simplicity and comfort.

150   FOXCONN HEADQUARTERS SHANGHAI

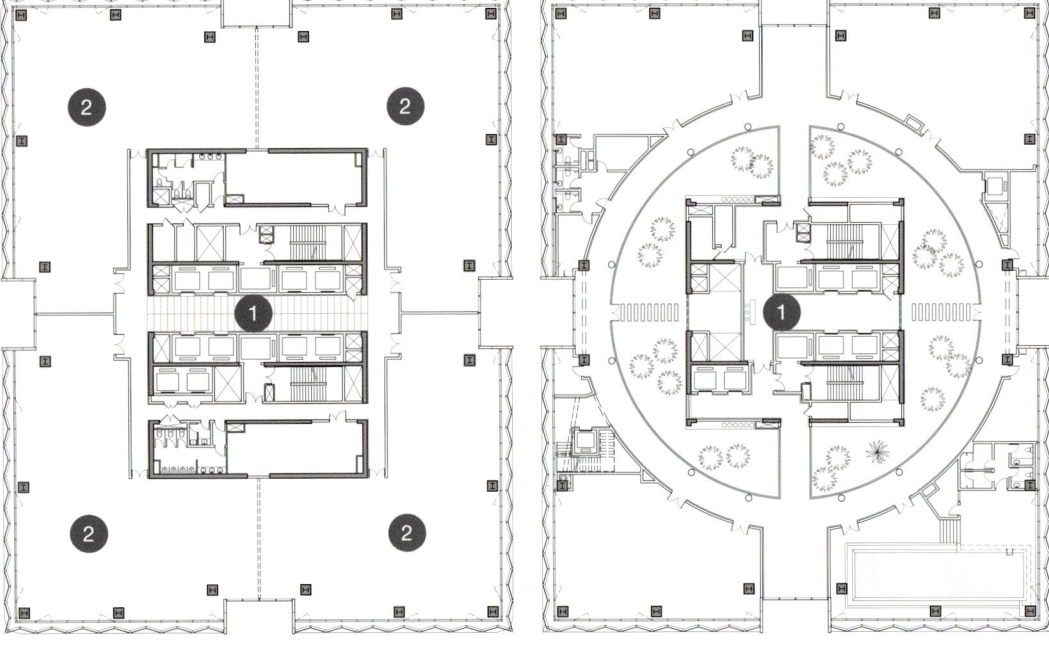

▲
Standing atop four basement levels, the building rises 21 stories above ground to a height of 95 meters. It is a steel-structured edifice, with a concrete core at the center of the tower.

▲
TYPICAL LOW ZONE FLOOR PLAN
1 Lift lobby
2 Office

▲
TYPICAL HIGH ZONE FLOOR PLAN

Sectional perspective through the rooftop multipurpose space and the ground-floor lobby.

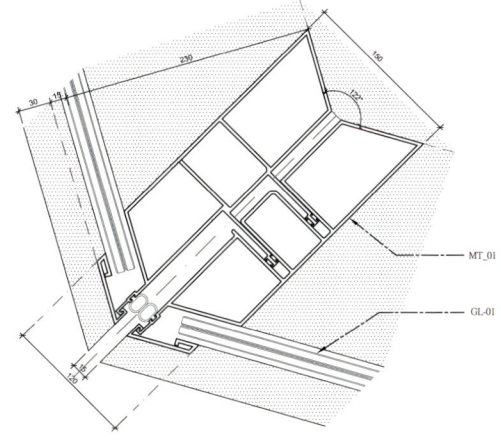
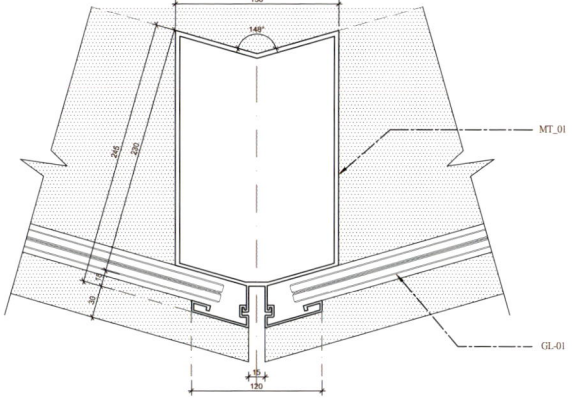
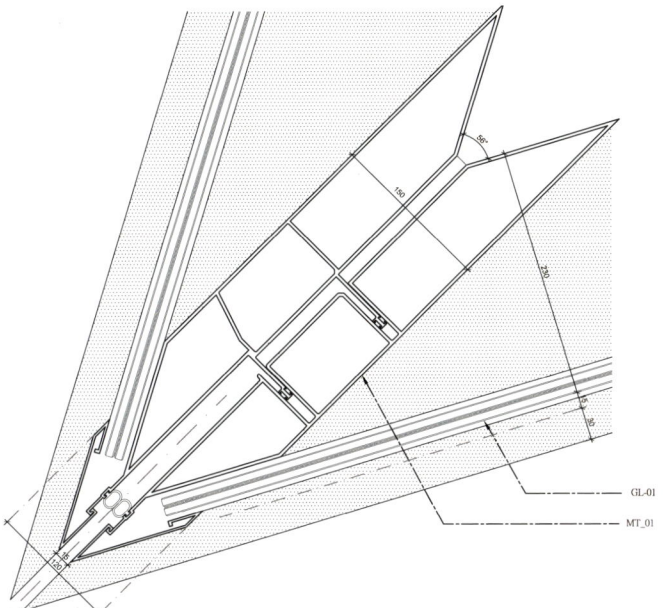
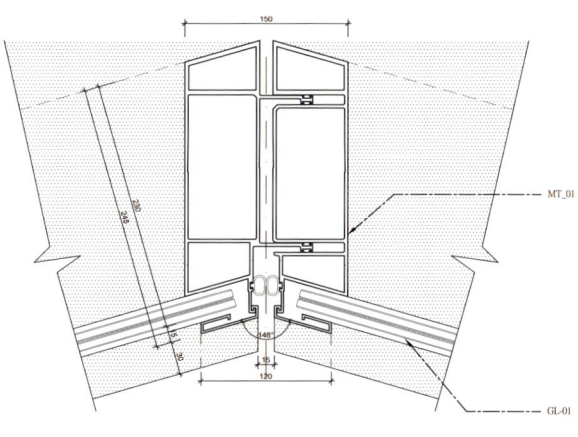

▲
FACADE DETAIL

During the day, the repeated V-shaped folds of the facade distort light and reflection to create a series of flamboyant displays; at nighttime, the building becomes the canvas for a spectacular light show, with the glowing details of the city mirroring the glittering reflections in the river below. The facade adopts a double-layer curtain-wall system with external ventilation, and movable louvers in the cavity are programmed to block direct sun, reducing heat gain and glare. The use of low-iron glass creates the impression of a crystal-clear finish, and its high reflectance value maximizes the penetration of natural light into the internal spaces.

The Foxconn Headquarters is a model of clarity and sustainability. It utilizes the advantages of a square layout to increase flexibility and efficiency with its internal spaces, and the architectural scale (together with the four-sided curtain-wall glass) allows the even distribution of natural light in the office areas. In addition, sustainable measures, such as solar panels, geothermal heat pumps, rainwater collection, and waste-water recycling, secured the building LEED Platinum certification, in line with Foxconn's emphasis on corporate social responsibility.

To the south, the tower steps back 46 meters from the main road to make space for an entrance plaza, where rows of trees in triangular planters provide vegetation and echo the geometric scheme of the facade. To the north, the podium cantilevers out to create a covered courtyard around a secondary entrance. Tree-lined walkways then run circling the site boundary, protecting pedestrians from the warm summer sun while also creating a friendly and pleasant urban space.

158 FOXCONN HEADQUARTERS SHANGHAI

TONG HSING ELECTRONICS

Completed year: 2023 | Location: Taoyuan, Taiwan

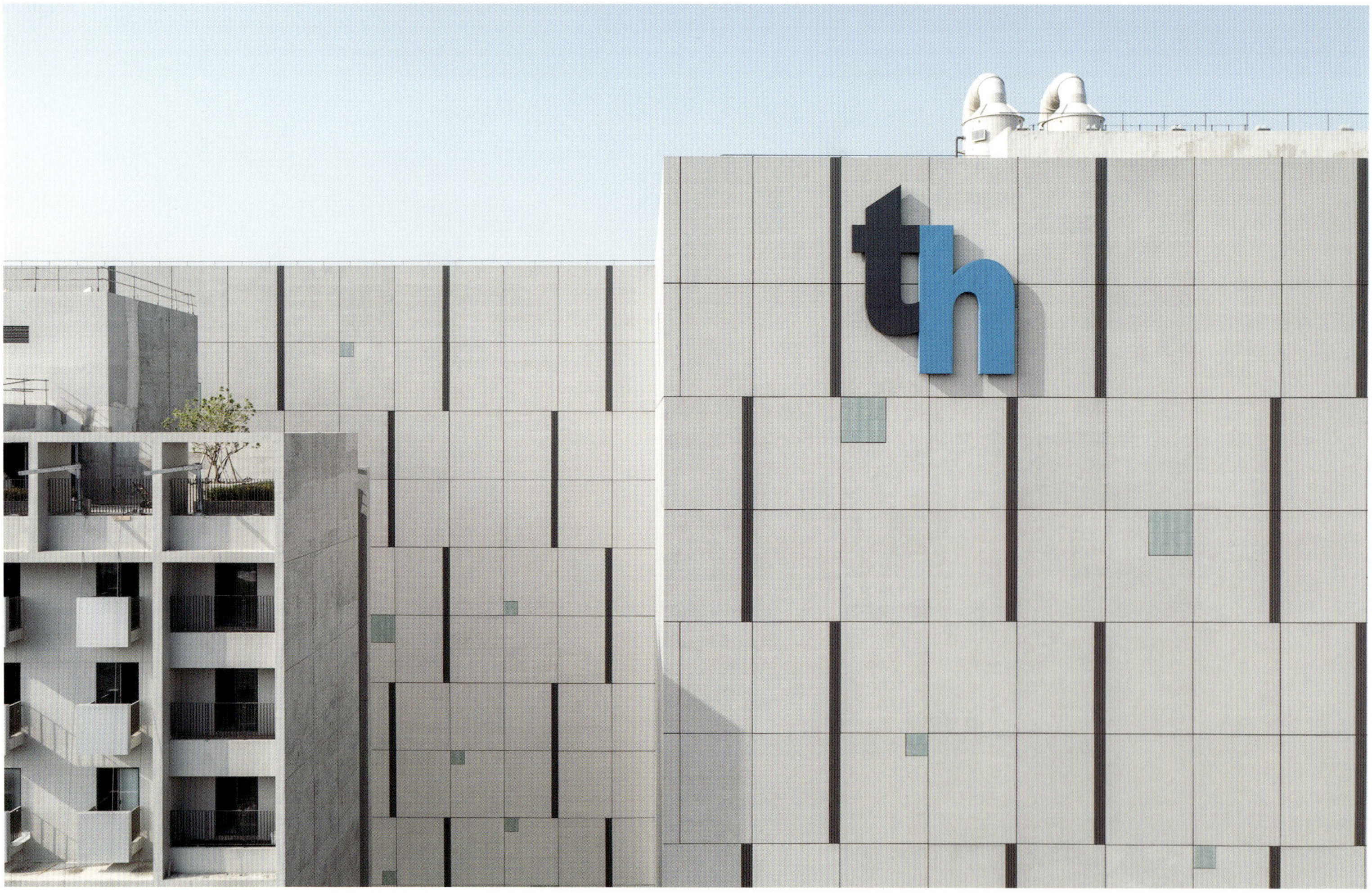

Client: Tong Hsing Electronic Industries, Ltd.
Area: 89,416 m²

Tong Hsing Electronics decided to build its new factory and corporate headquarters in the Bade District of Taoyuan City, due to its proximity to the existing Yingge plant, thereby increasing flexibility in terms of production capacity, technology, and workforce. The new site covers 16,700 square meters, with a total floor area of 89,000 square meters, which encompasses the headquarters building and the fabrication plant, as well as staff accommodation.

The headquarters building is an almost entirely red square box, 50 meters tall, and punctured by irregularly placed square openings of varying sizes, giving the building a modest degree of playfulness. Extending out at a right angle to the rear of this is the fabrication plant. This is a gray rectangular block, its single-color facade similarly broken up by an arrangement of vertical louvers and square terracotta tiles. To achieve a more sustainable solution, while also minimizing construction time and costs, the plant was clad in precast modular concrete panels.

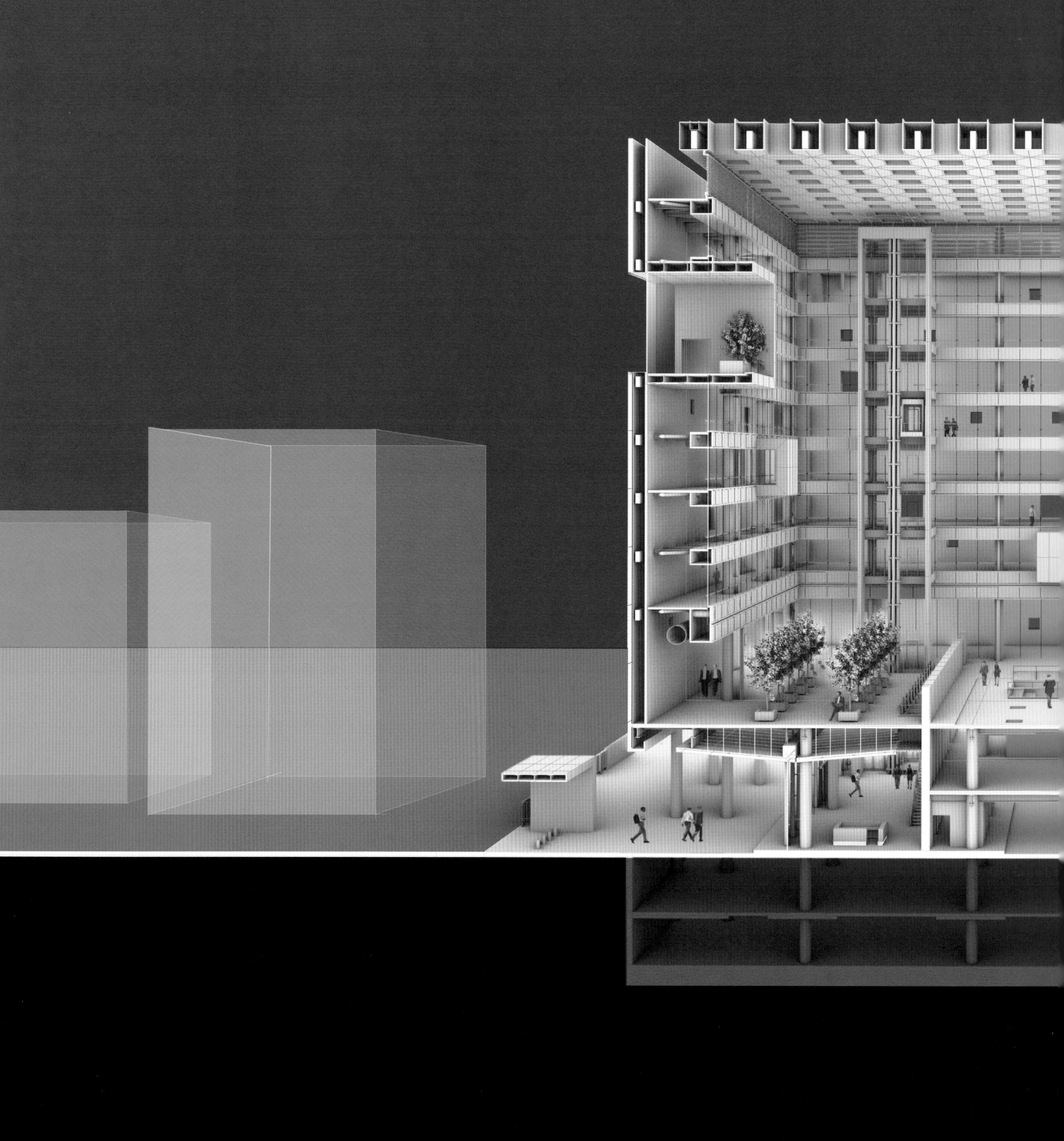

Sectional perspective through the light-filled office atrium.

The highlight of the site is the 10-story atrium at the heart of the headquarters building, which provides a pleasant internal courtyard where employees can relax, socialize, or attend corporate events. Natural light filters through the waffle slab above, bathing the space and its occupants in sunlight, while foliage hanging from wire mesh boxes, together with rows of trees at the lower level, adds softening greenery.

Numerous solid boxes with large openings protrude out into the courtyard, creating informal meeting spaces, while in the interior, the main circulation and meeting spaces are configured around the atrium, left visible behind glass walls. Horizontal timber bands then run around the perimeter at each level. The generous use of transparent partitions allows visual connections between occupants on different floors, and encourages an open and lively work environment.

168 TONG HSING ELECTRONICS

◀
Square insets and protruding balconies of varying sizes create rhythmic patterns on the facades, while also providing spaces that greatly improve the living and working conditions of employees.

TSMC HSINCHU R&D CENTER

Completed year: 2023 | Location: Hsinchu, Taiwan

◂ Seen from the entrance, the simplicity of a cylindrical mass and a linear water fountain complement the geometric volume of the main building.

Client: Taiwan Semiconductor Manufacturing Company, Ltd. (TSMC)

The Taiwan Semiconductor Manufacturing Company's R&D center is located in the Hsinchu Science Park—Northern Taiwan's leading industrial park. The center's design adopts a logical approach to incorporating a high-performance technology plant with a modular workspace. It can accommodate up to 8,000 engineers and it contributes to the development of new production lines for one of the world's leading semiconductor manufacturing firms.

The 30-meter height difference that existed on the site presented a great challenge. In order to reduce its visual impact and turn the unfavorable to their advantage, KYA placed the taller office building, with a stepped basement, in the center—the lowest point of the site, serving also as the core circulation space between the two fabs to either side. This arrangement improves workflow and efficiency by encouraging interaction between the two production bases. The cultivated atmosphere of the office quarters also creates a pleasing contrast to the simple geometric forms of the fabrication plants.

The offices look onto a large atrium measuring 160 meters long, 40 meters wide, and 47 meters high. Sky bridges cut through the void at several levels, offering

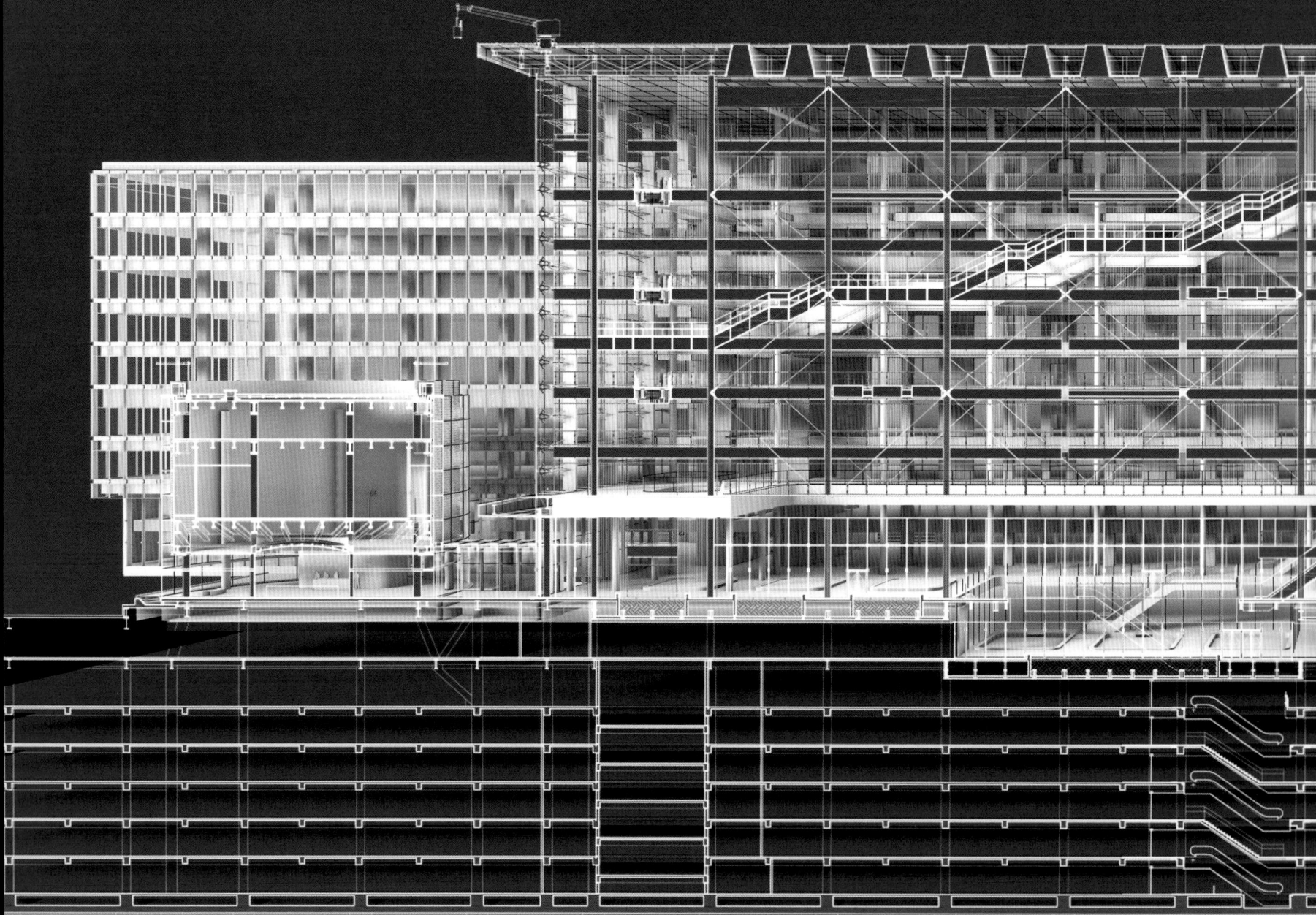

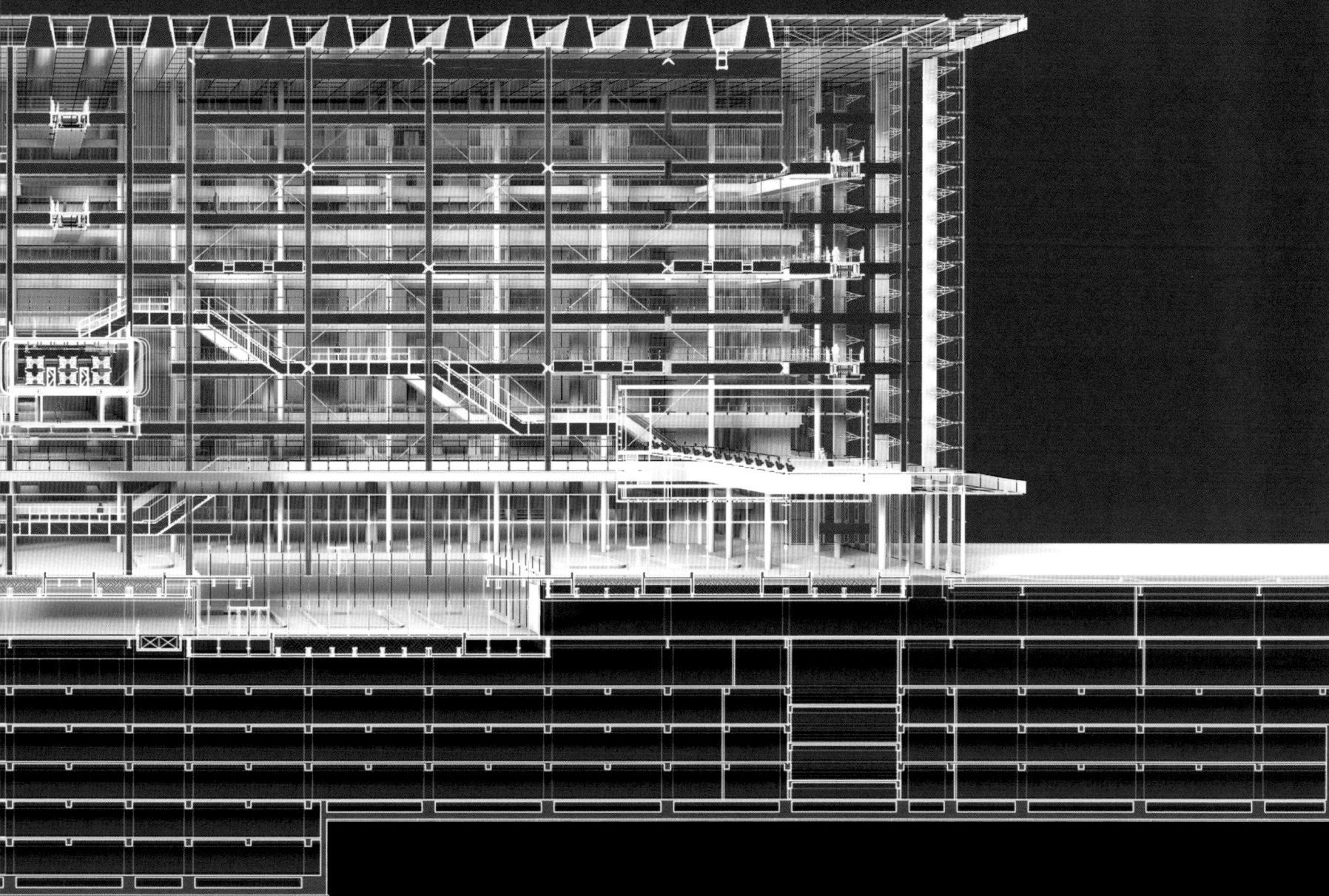

elevated shortcuts from one side of the building to another. Together the height, open corridors, central water feature, and decorative timber panels create a bright and calming atmosphere. Natural light is brought in through sky openings and an expanse of low-E laminated curtain-wall glass. The height of the atrium also encourages stack ventilation, drawing fresh air in near the bottom and expelling stale air at the top, transforming this technical facility into a pleasant and sustainable workplace.

In response to extreme weather fluctuations in the region, two retention ponds were planned for the northern and southern parts of the site, to accommodate surface runoff from heavy rains. A handful of sustainability measures were also put in place to achieve LEED Gold certification, including the installation of solar panels on top of the office building, the recycling of condensation from the fabs for the cooling towers, the use of energy-saving and heat-reduction materials both on the exterior and interior, as well as various devices and fixtures to significantly reduce pollution and water consumption.

The center satisfies TSMC's request for a green and friendly work environment on a highly efficient production site, primed to achieve sustainable growth and to continue to push boundaries in the semiconductor industry.

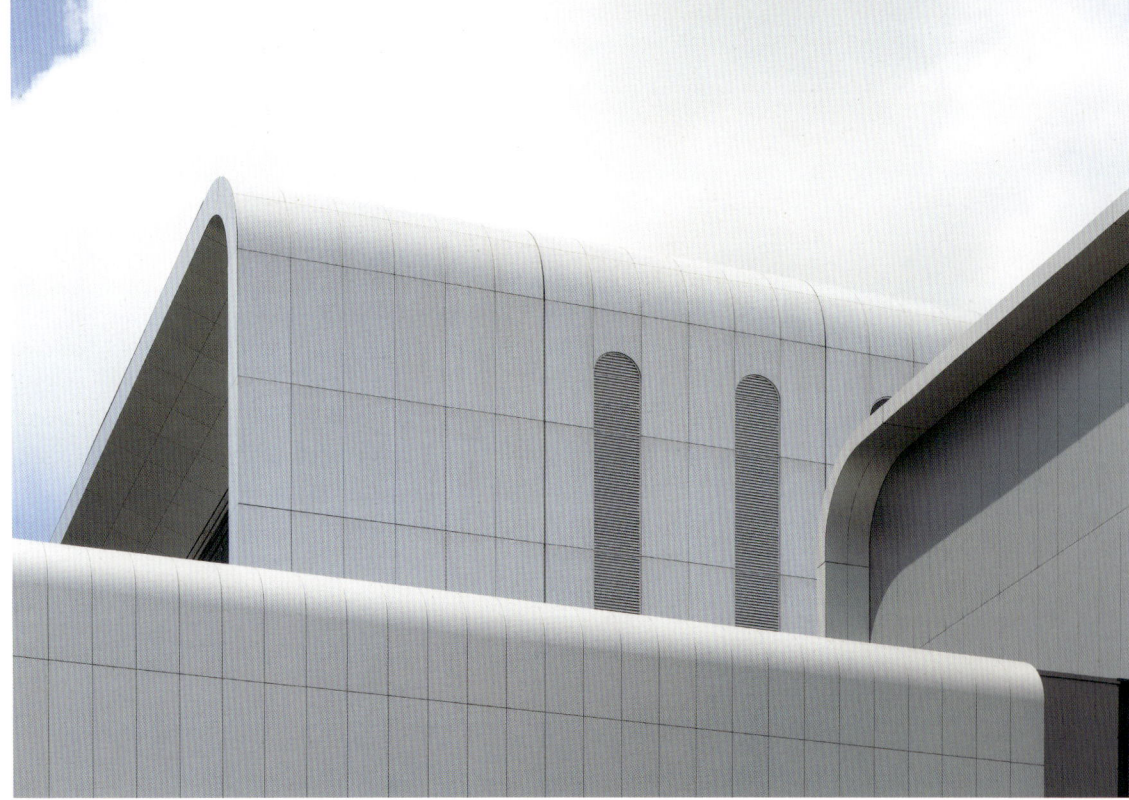

▲
The great mass of the building, the handsome silvery coat it wears, and the capsule-like windows on its skin make the plant seem as if straight out of a high-tech movie scene.

CHINA DEVELOPMENT HEADQUARTERS

Completed year: 2020 | Location: Taipei, Taiwan

CHINA DEVELOPMENT HEADQUARTERS

Client: China Life Insurance Co., Ltd.
Area: 81,495 m²

The China Development Headquarters rises 18 stories above ground and plunges 5 stories below. The main entrance, which faces Taipei's Dunhua North Road, serves the offices on the first 12 floors and the executive suites on the top floor. A second entry to one side provides access to the five-star hotel housed on floors 14 to 17, isolating its circulation from the offices for security and management purposes.

Time has left its mark on three old trees—preserved from the original site—that silently stand guard over the new occupant. Around them, a well-executed landscape design assembles plants, pools, benches, and pavements to create an open and fluid space for the public to enjoy. After dark, the glass cube facing it glows like a light box, catching the attention of passersby on foot and in cars, and injecting new energy into the nighttime cityscape.

Sustainable measures played a major role in the building's design. Retention ponds were dotted around the site to regulate the microclimate, recycle and reuse rainwater, and establish a water-diversion system. The project also included the systematic control of sensor lights and electric double-layer curtain louvers to achieve the desired daily energy savings. Together these decisions have produced a modern office complex that performs well and is highly sustainable.

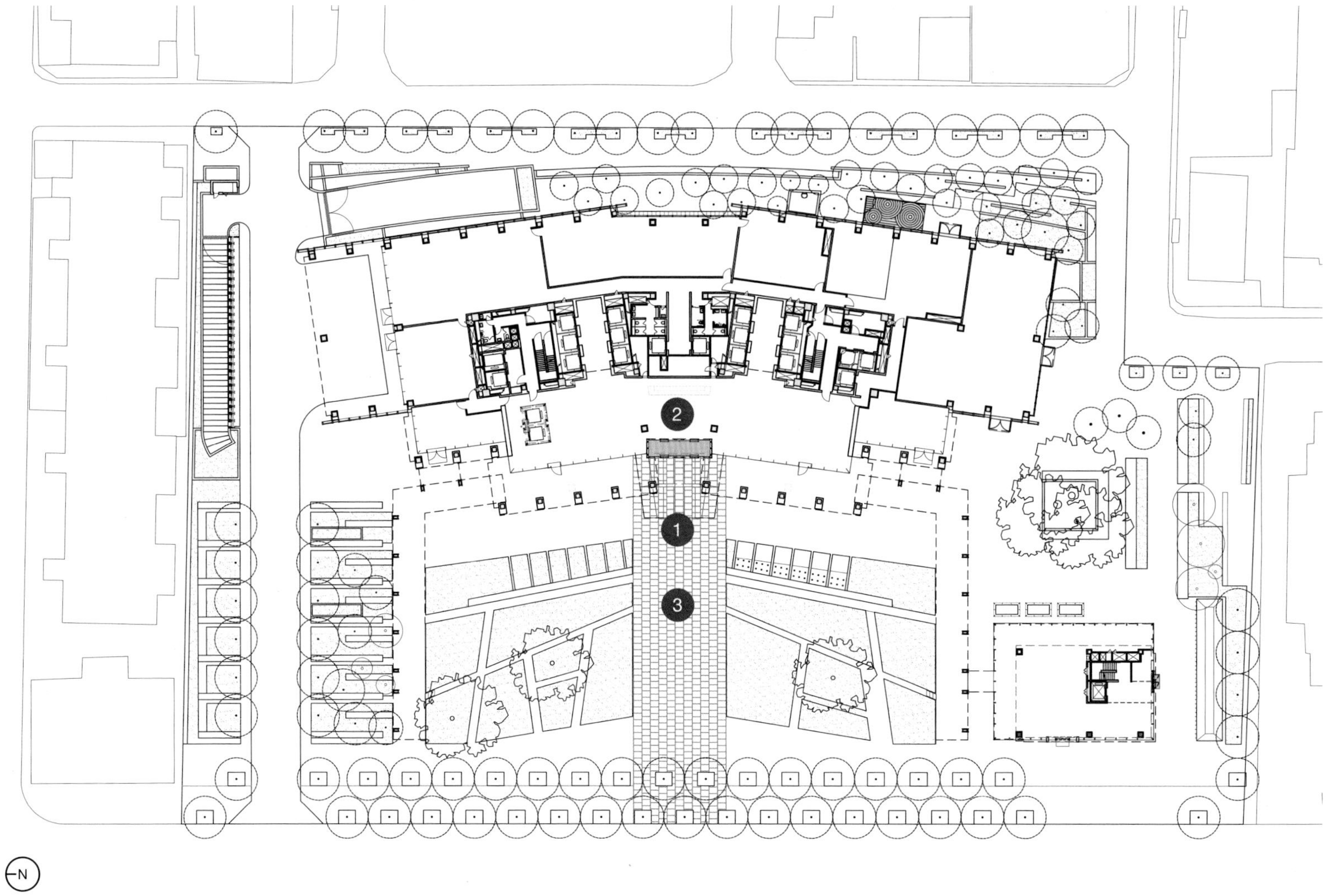

186 CHINA DEVELOPMENT HEADQUARTERS

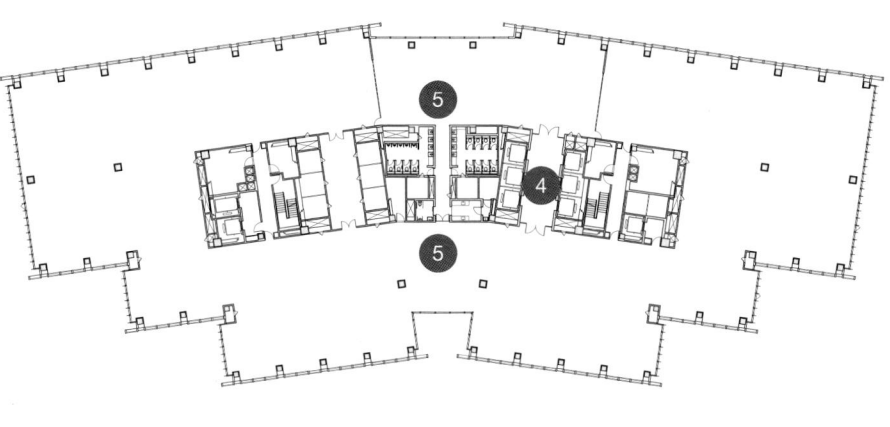

▲ GROUND FLOOR PLAN

◀ TYPICAL OFFICE FLOOR PLAN

▲ TYPICAL HOTEL FLOOR PLAN

1 Entrance
2 Lobby
3 Plaza
4 Lift lobby
5 Office

▶ The building steps back from the busy Dunhua North Road, opening up much of the ground level to an expansive park, a space that the client gifted to the public.

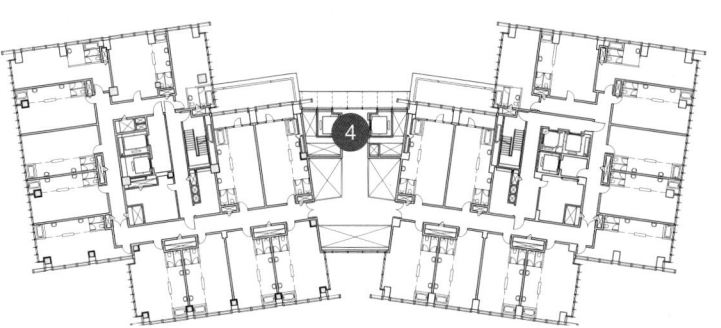

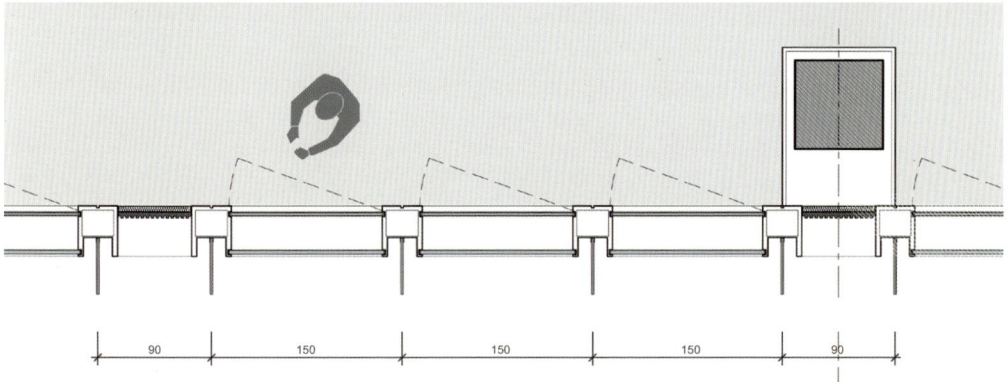
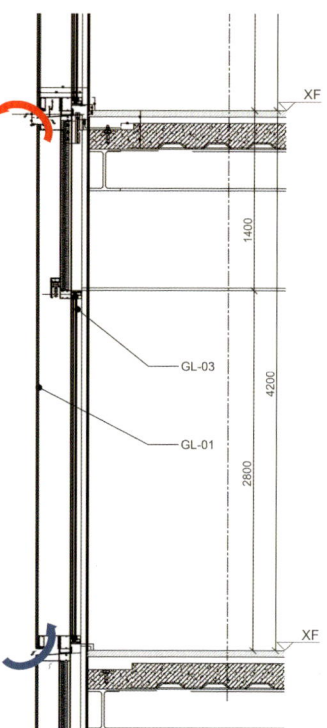

◄
FACADE DETAIL

◄
The tower is coated in a low-E, super-white laminated double skin, its great mass camouflaged in the clear reflection of the sky above.

From the 14th floor, the building steps back to accommodate the hotel's pool and sky garden, its mass wrapped in a curtain wall glass system that appears exceedingly light in color, due to its high reflectance value. The team looked into the low-iron glass with a reflective coating that RPBW employed for the Shard in London, which allows its pinnacle to dissolve into the sky. Here, KYA opted for a low-emissivity, super-white laminated glass and ceramic-fused glass in combination with gray granite to create a shimmering crystalline effect that combines transparency and immateriality. Its lightness is further enhanced by single panes of glass projecting up to screen rooftop services, which give the building a feathered silhouette against the sky. As with the Foxconn Shanghai headquarters, KYA took the low-carbon approach of a double-curtain wall installation—running east to west—that encloses mechanized blinds to mitigate heat and glare from the late afternoon sun on the tower and side pavilions.

JOY CITY CHONGQING

Completed year: 2023 | Location: Chongqing, China

Client: Grandjoy Holdings Group Co., Ltd.
Area: 352,887 m²

This mixed-use project turns a challenging site to its advantage, creating a commercial center with great character and appeal. To the north, the commercial podium and towers are clad in glass and silver-gray aluminum panels, giving them a light-hearted urban simplicity. Square masses of varying surface finishes then thrust into the podium from various angles,

creating an exciting juxtaposition of solids and voids at the lower levels.

The podium stretches across two plots, maximizing the buildable area to 180 meters north to south, and 150 meters east to west. It rises seven stories to reach a height of 42 meters.

To the south, a complex series of terraces provide zones for art, performance, and commercial activities. Unlike the view in the other three directions, the south looks out onto a landscaped valley, used by locals for recreation—a green zone that sits in strong contrast to the densely packed high-rises and major transportation hub to the north.

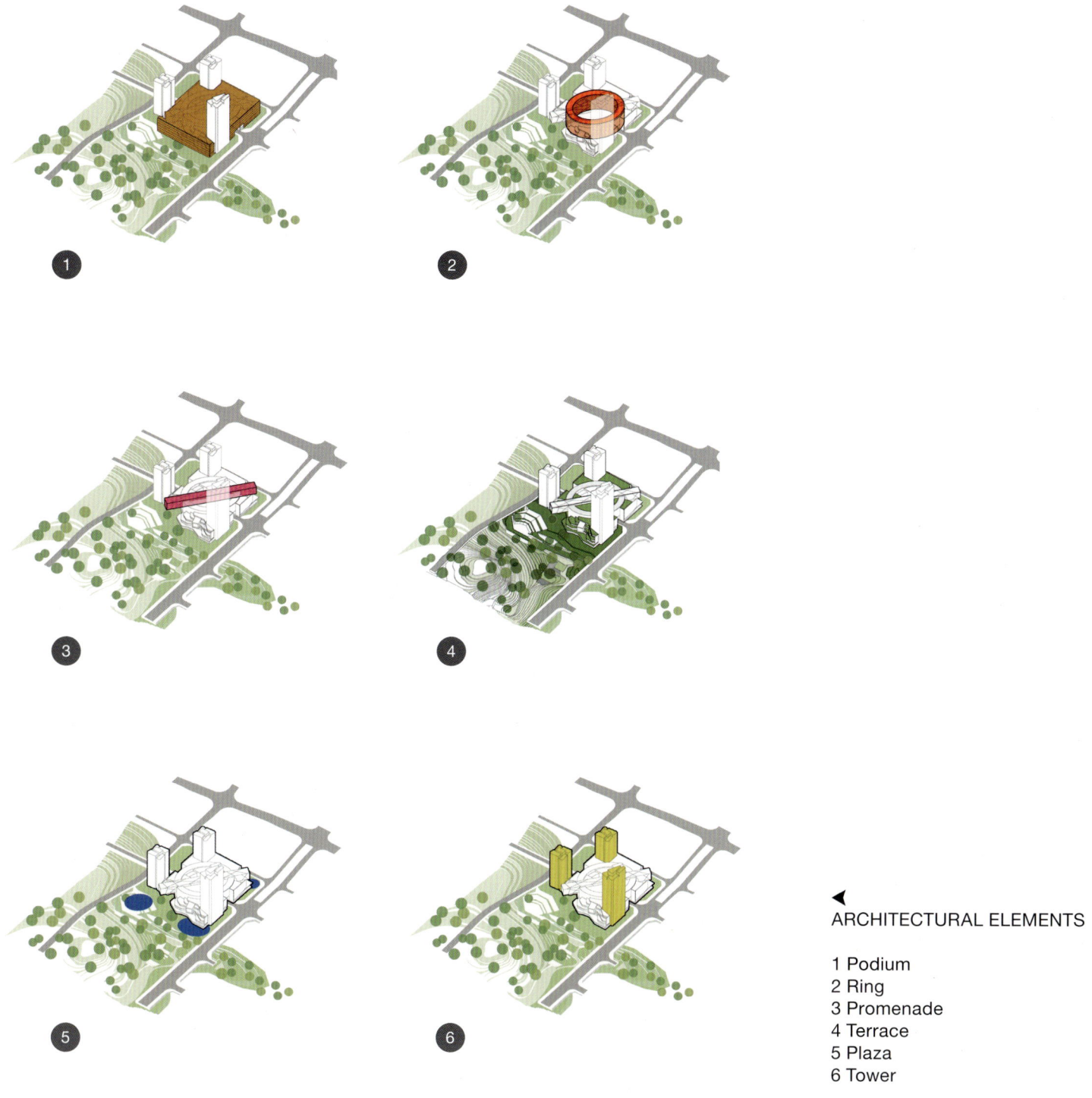

◀
ARCHITECTURAL ELEMENTS

1 Podium
2 Ring
3 Promenade
4 Terrace
5 Plaza
6 Tower

Joy City Chongqing covers 46,000 square meters, with a total floor area of 355,000 square meters, of which 145,000 are the commercial podium, while the three office and residential towers combined account for another 94,000. The two podium masses, sited at the intersection of two subway lines and ruthlessly sliced in half by a four-lane arterial road, are crucially linked by an elliptical circulation ring and an oversized rectangular tube.

The landscaped terraces to the south lead down in stepped fashion toward the natural parkland beyond, bordered by a scenic dam that was increased to a width of 50 meters. Flowerbed-lined paths, elevated bridges, and stairways weave through this area, constituting a city park of its own.

Sectional perspective through the 200-meter-long multipurpose corridor, the

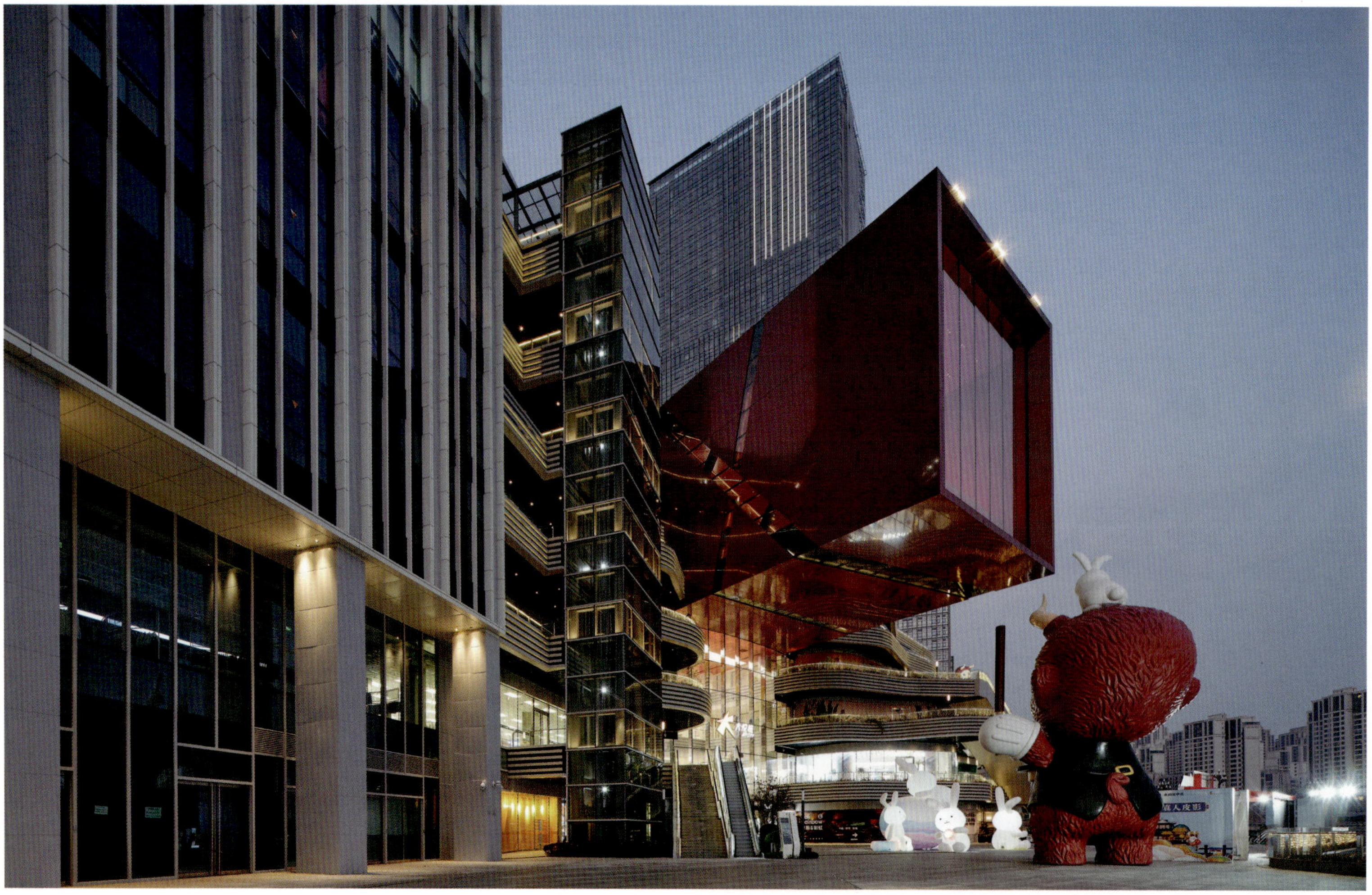

◀
5TH FLOOR PLAN

1 Tube
2 Ring
3 Retail
4 Restaurants

 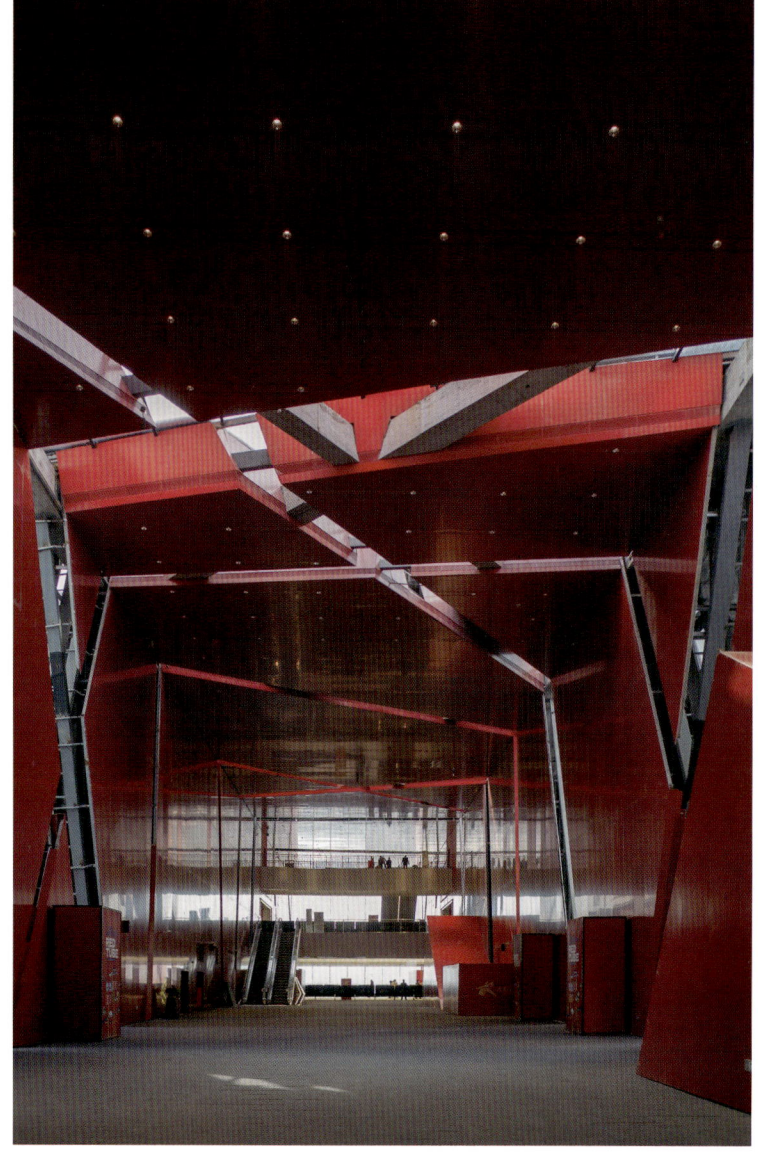

The interior design then continues the same theme, bringing elements of nature indoors, including fabricated mountain paths, hills, waterfalls, and gorges. Five unique zones further distinguish this from more conventional retail complexes. The first is the Canyon Walkway, extending the concept of a mountain city, while the Floating Stone recreates the famous mountain ranges and rivers of Chongqing. The Special Cave simulates a science-fiction environment, the Gourmet Market provides a mouth-watering array of local cuisines, and the Tube Corridor provides a fusion of art and technology.

The two circulation routes linking the two commercial podiums are positioned one on top of the other, with the elliptical ring at the lower level, and the tubular corridor above it, oriented north to south. The corridor is finished in a vivid red, sliced diagonally at various points and at varying angles, in a manner that mirrors the forms of the terraces to the south, softening the boundary between interior and exterior. It spans 200 meters along its length, and is three stories tall, providing a suitable space for special events and exhibitions. At either end, the corridor cantilevers out by 20 meters, overlooking the city to the north and the valley to the south, thereby visually connecting the urbanscape with the natural environment.

FAR EASTERN
RETAIL COMPLEX

Completed year: 2019 | Location: Taipei, Taiwan

Client: Far Eastern Department Store Co., Ltd.
Area: 78,192 m²

Another of the six buildings on Songren Road designed by KYA, the Far Eastern retail complex gleams proudly in the southeastern corner of Taipei's Xinyi Commercial District. Gray aluminum volumes stack on top of one another like gift boxes under a Christmas tree, with their rounded corners providing a futuristic appearance as well as a reduction in wind load. Balconies offer observation points at various levels, and a protruding glass tube adds a visual highlight both externally and internally. In contrast to other shopping centers in the district, this stands out like a work of the future, drawing visitors into a world of the latest technology and trends. Set amidst an urban jungle of cutting-edge corporate buildings and retail complexes, the Far Eastern property's setbacks and clean lines give visual relief. The building also allows for a generous plaza to the south, providing precious space for leisure and relaxation in a district where land is at a premium.

The facade makes use of contrasting tones of light and dark silver to differentiate between the variously sized boxes, while recessed composite glass creates shadowy gaps between them, giving the illusion that they are floating, kept apart by an imaginary magnetic force. Although the building as a whole creates a futuristic impression, its silver and transparent containers connect it to the surrounding commercial environment, while vintage design elements link it to the older parts of the city.

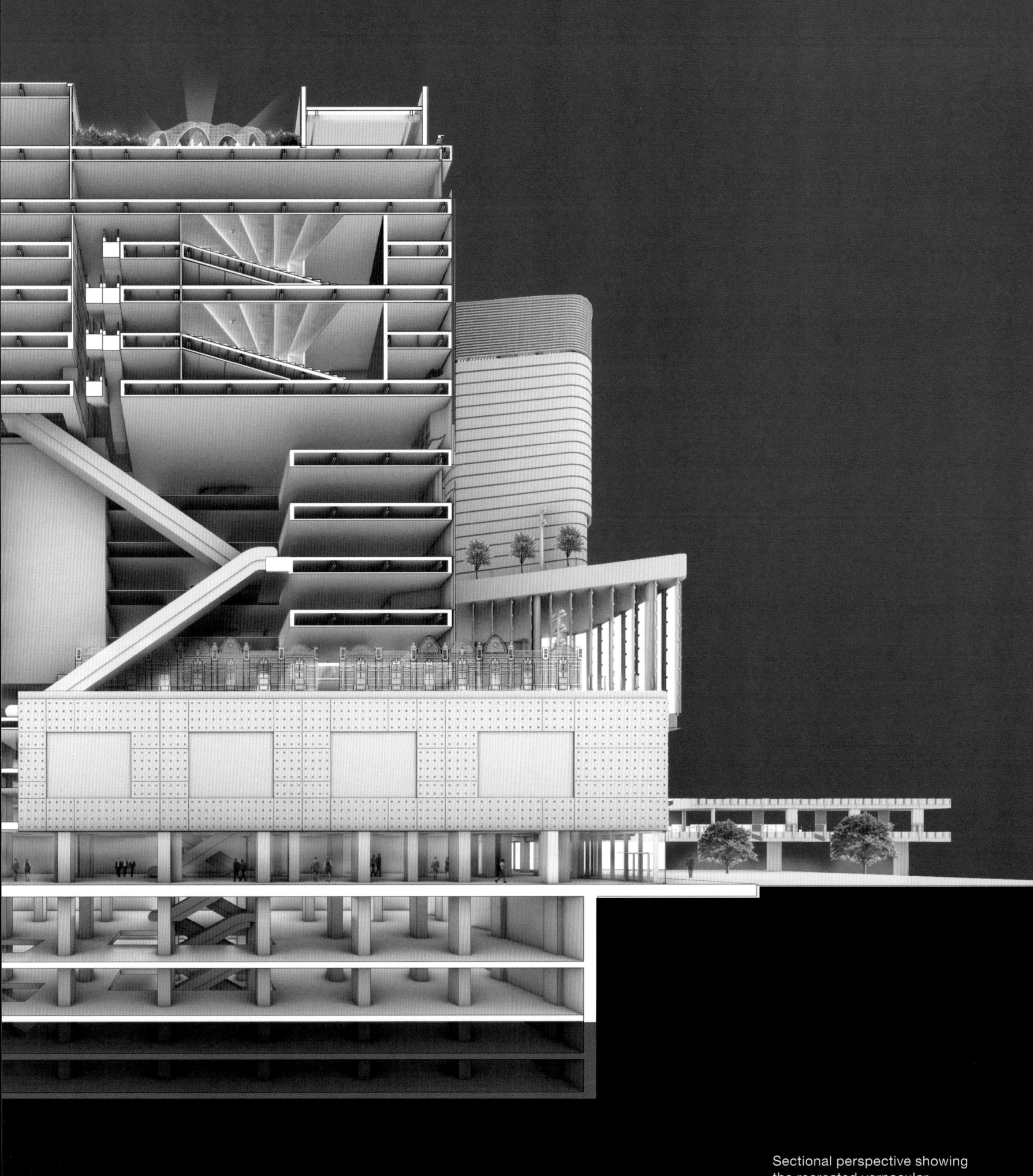

Sectional perspective showing the recreated vernacular streetscape on Level 4, the movie theaters, and the express escalators.

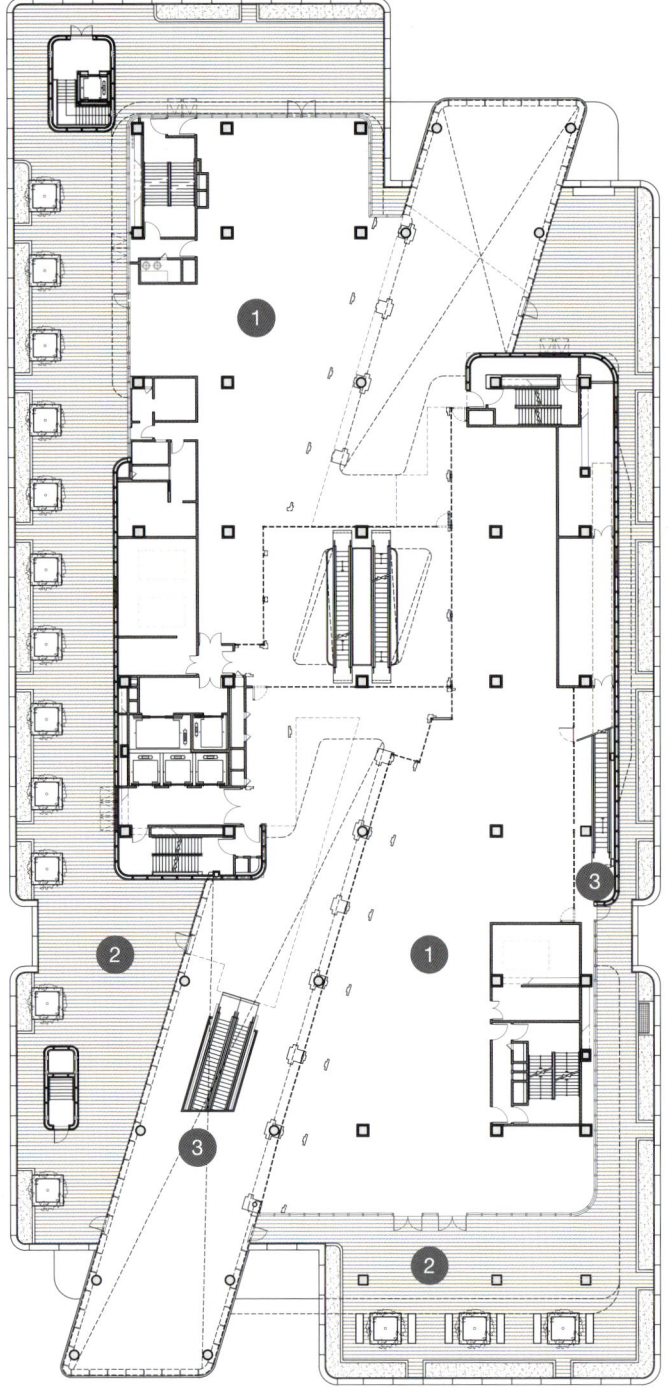

◀
4TH FLOOR PLAN

1 Restaurant
2 Outdoor terrace
3 Express escalator

The box arrangement is based on four vertical zones, determined by function. The "boutique" area within the bottom perforated panels includes Levels 1 to 3; the "food and leisure" section in the lower silver boxes spans Levels 4 to 6; the upper metal cases, which hold the "health and fitness" zone, span Levels 7 to 9; the "movie" zone extends from Level 10 to 13; and the six rooftop restaurants, with extensive views of the shopping district, are located on Level 14. In addition to elevators and conventional floor-to-floor escalators, three express escalators were installed to deliver customers more directly to particular zones.

Each express escalator offers a unique journey, building anticipation for what is to come. The first shortcut passes through a "cosmic" zone, with dim blue lights arranged like constellations in the ceiling, which is in sharp contrast to the traditional street scene that visitors encounter as they exit. The second and third express elevators travel through a narrow portion of the west facade, which is punctured by a diagonal slice running parallel to the slope of the second escalator. Movie-goers are sent directly to the cinema ticket office via the third express elevator—a dimmed, tube-like space that allows their eyes to adjust in readiness for the darkness of the screening rooms.

▶ The interior highlight of the project is the replica street scene on Level 4, based on Taipei's historic Dihua Street. Wrapped in a protruding glass tube, the decorative brick facade, balustrades decorated with Chinese motifs, and shop-sign calligraphy take on an almost surreal appearance behind the faint reflection of the sky.

Client: United Daily News Co., Ltd.
Area: 75,310 m²

Three architectural elements make up the elegant and modernized edifice of the United Daily News building: an eight-meter-high lobby, fully glazed and set back behind steel-clad columns; 18 floors of offices, shaded by vertical screen-printed glass fins on the wider sides, and wrapped by horizontal aluminum bands on the shorter ends; and a 10-story residential block at the top. The three elements are stacked one on top of the other, with privacy and quality of views increasing in line with ascent.

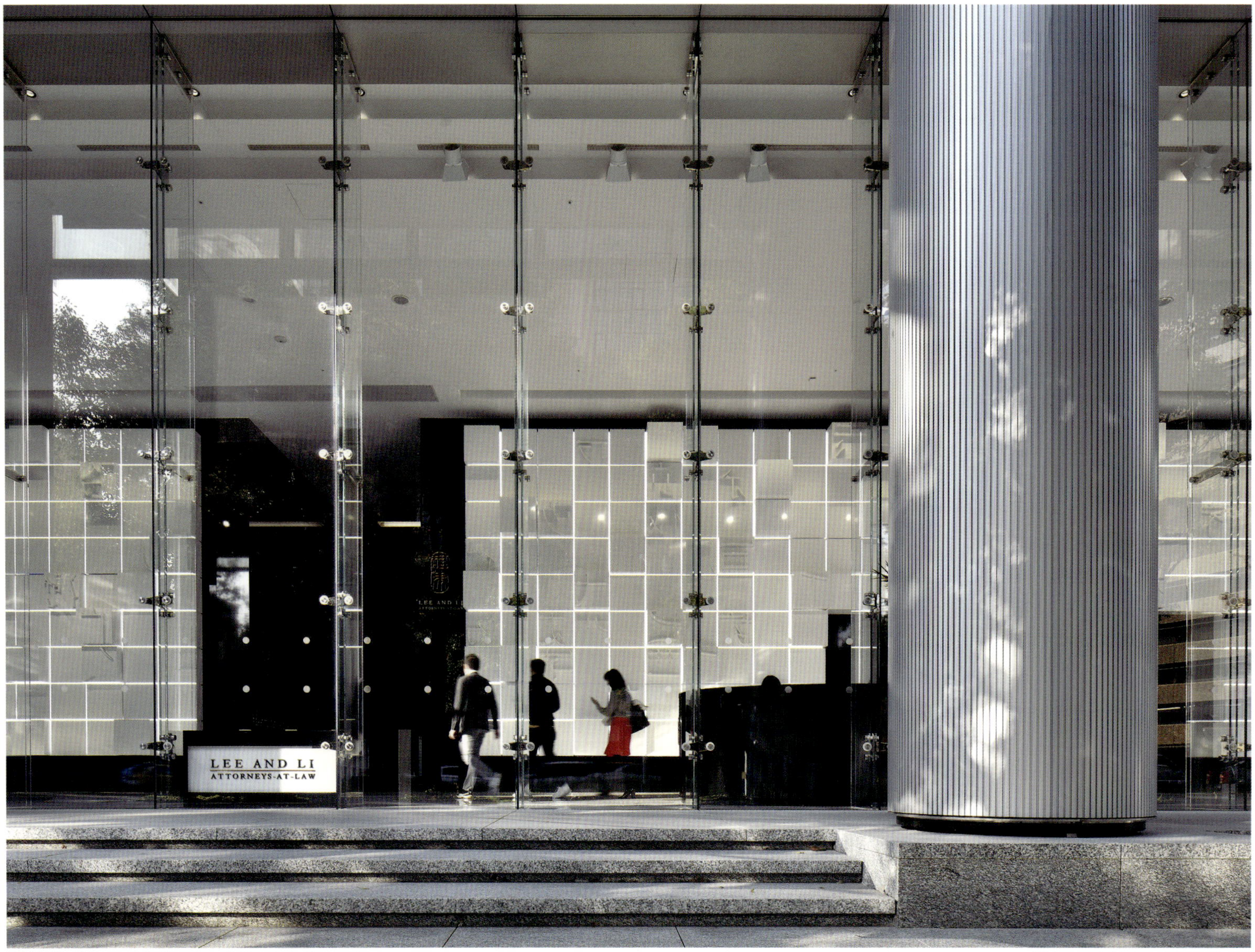

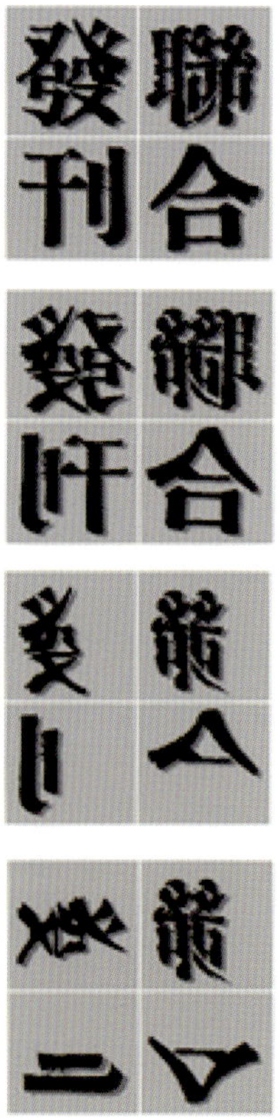

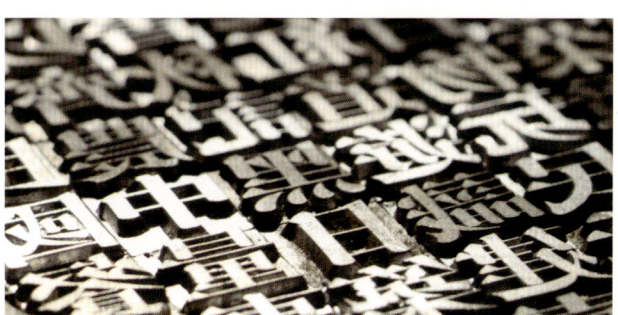

Multiple allusions to movable type hint at the former occupant of the site—the United Daily News. The rear wall of the lobby is covered with large relief sculptures of Chinese characters, transforming a plain wall into a captivating display of protruding and recessing blocks. Likewise, the stone blocks that complete the water feature at the southeast corner of the building take the form of giant printing blocks, with a hidden mechanism creating vapor, as if concealing the secrets of ancient China's printing technology behind a misty veil. Though such methods have long been superseded by modern technology, these physical reminders give the building its distinct identity, and pay tribute to one of the most significant achievements of Chinese civilization.

Sandwiched between the busy Zhongxiao East Road and a quiet alley, the tower divides its arrival circulation into north and south at ground level. The office lobby faces the lively street to the south, drawing in multiple visitors and clients from its bustling pedestrian traffic. The apartment entrance opens onto the serene passageway to the north, giving residents maximum privacy from this buzzing commercial district. Trees shield the building from traffic on three sides, and beside the main entrance to the apartments, a discrete ramp leads down to several levels of subterranean parking, covered by a decorative canopy. The separate lobbies not only alleviate security controls by restricting access, but also increase elevator efficiency through vertical zoning, dividing the tower into high (residential), mid (office), and low (office) zones. Between the offices and the residential zone there is also a double-height event space, shared by both residents and workers.

RESIDENTIAL

EVENT SPACE

OFFICE

GARDEN
RESIDENTIAL
ENTRY ▶

◀ CITY BLVD.
OFFICE
ENTRY

Cross section through the office and residential units.

Views from the apartments take in the two most prominent and most contrasting features of Taipei—its central business district, and the mountain ranges that surround the Taipei Basin. The units enjoy unobstructed views of the man-made world to the south, and vistas of the natural world beyond to the north.

Playing off the United Daily News is a 24-story apartment tower on the next block, placed at the other end of the boulevard and employing a similar language of stepped balconies and aluminum trims. It is from such simple juxtapositions—of tall and short, wide and narrow, vertical and horizontal thrusts—that lively streets are made. Setbacks and jutting balconies enrich the profiles of both towers, hinting at the shared bloodlines between these two simple-looking yet intricately detailed buildings. The drama of the contrast, and the harmony of their constituent parts, demonstrate KYA's skill in urban planning, and the cachet that impeccable finishes and detailing give to a luxury development.

HUA NAN BANK

Completed year: 2014 Location: Taipei, Taiwan

Client: Hua Nan Commercial Bank Ltd.
Area: 51,750 m²

Most of the Hua Nan Bank's neighbors down Songren Road have towers growing out of podiums that gradually step back from the street, but this building rises 27 stories from a straight-faced three-story podium. As the German architectural critic Ulf Meyer wrote, it "follows the modernist paradigm of a solitary tower on a plaza, which does not do much to animate the streetscapes around it." However, the erection of Mies van der Rohe's Seagram Building in New York demonstrated the effectiveness of this approach as a way of maximizing the visibility of the main elevation.

The exoskeleton of the bank is clad in brown granite imported from Brazil, a color that unites it with the KYA-designed Kelti Tower to its north, and native plants are dotted around the foot of the bank, irrigated solely by rain and gray water.

Exposed structure and balconies as sunshading devices and thermal buffers.

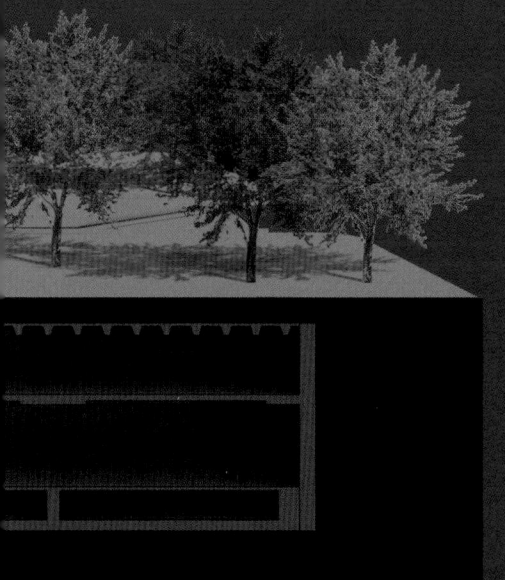

Sectional perspective through the lobby, the sky gardens, and the office spaces.

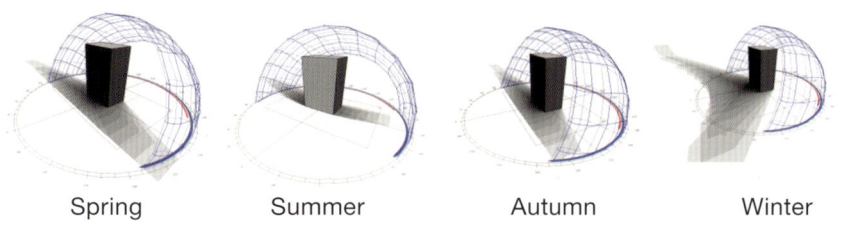

| Spring | Summer | Autumn | Winter |

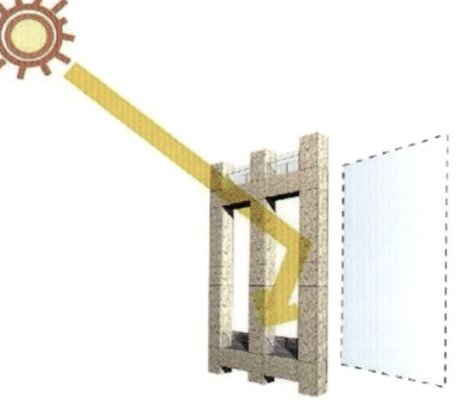

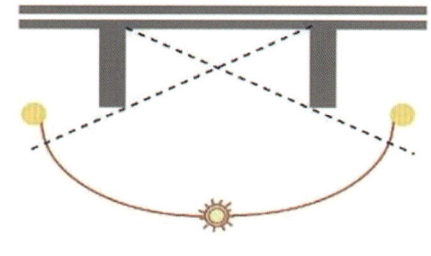

The urban planning laws of Xinyi District posed great challenges to the sustainability strategy of the building. The east–west orientation of the site, with the main elevation facing west, went against the fundamental principles of a conventional "green" architecture, but the design team managed to acquire gold ratings in both LEED and EEWH—in particular, with the use of narrow floor plates that allow daylight to reach deep into the building, and a green roof that retains water for recycling. Rainwater is harvested for irrigation, and gray water is reused for flushing toilets. The "sky

gardens" act as thermal buffers that reduce solar gain from the west-facing facade, each complemented by a large ceiling fan and one of eight varieties of tree to aid destratification.

The architectural characteristics that set the Hua Nan Bank apart can only be fully appreciated upon exploration of its interior, from the delicate beauty of the sky gardens, to the plants, high ceilings, balconies, Chinese-style louvers, and various other environmentally friendly details throughout. Together, they deliver an exciting new standard for high-rise design in Taiwan.

A HILLTOP CAMPUS

Design year: 2018 | Location: Jiangsu, China

A HILLTOP CAMPUS

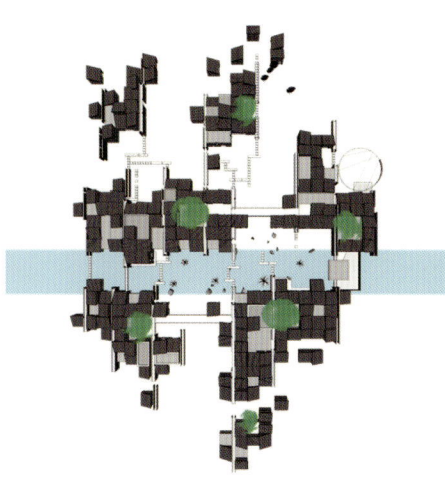

Area: 68,038 m²

This global high-tech company turned down the typical curtain-wall high-rise in an urban center, deciding instead to construct a hilltop business base that pays great respect to Chinese vernacular architecture. This nature-filled site is sandwiched between tea plantations and a forest of large camphor trees, and offers stunning views of the mountains on all sides. The goal was to integrate buildings and nature, minimizing the loss of the original landscape. The KYA team responded with a high-tech office layout wrapped in a reinterpreted traditional Jiangnan village—the region south of the Yangtze River.

The coming together of the man-made and the natural marked an integral part of the design brief. Buildings with white walls and pitched tiled roofs—

a tip of the hat to vernacular Jiangnan architecture—are positioned along a central canal between the forest and the plantation. They sit carefully in an area of gentler slopes, refraining from uprooting the existing landscape and planting in a campus as a replacement. These traditional-looking houses face the mountain and flow down the site's ungraded contours. The paths in between, where employees stroll about, belong to the forest, tea farms, and running stream that were already there. This project also utilizes natural elements to their fullest, bringing in as much daylight, fresh air, and rain as possible, for illumination, ventilation, and water consumption. Buildings and nature therefore integrate not only in terms of architectural configuration, but also more practically, in terms of environmental strategies.

Sectional perspective through the social hub, the performance hall, and the sports hall (from left to right).

244 A HILLTOP CAMPUS

◀
GROUND FLOOR PLAN

Layout of a campus within the mountains, cut through by a central canal that connects a series of small office units.

1 Entrance
2 Lobby
3 Conference
4 Exhibition
5 Office
6 Library
7 Canteen
8 Hub
9 Waterscape
10 Tea garden

▶ A tea plantation was preserved on site to retain this portion of existing landscape.

CHANGHUA
HIGH-SPEED RAIL STATION

Completed year: 2015   Location: Changhua, Taiwan

248 CHANGHUA HIGH-SPEED RAIL STATION

Client: Taiwan High Speed Rail Corporation
Area: 22,174 m²

This sleek embodiment of the spirit of high-speed travel provides a gateway to rice paddies and floriculture of Changhua County. The design of the station and its landscaping are intertwined, with vegetation, water, and paving revealed both at eye-level and from a bird's-eye view, and expansive spans of glazed facade allowing views to penetrate both ways. This "greenhouse" scheme also permits vistas into the surrounding countryside, reaching as far as the city of Tianzhong, ensuring that the natural beauty of the region leaves a memorable mark on travelers and passersby alike.

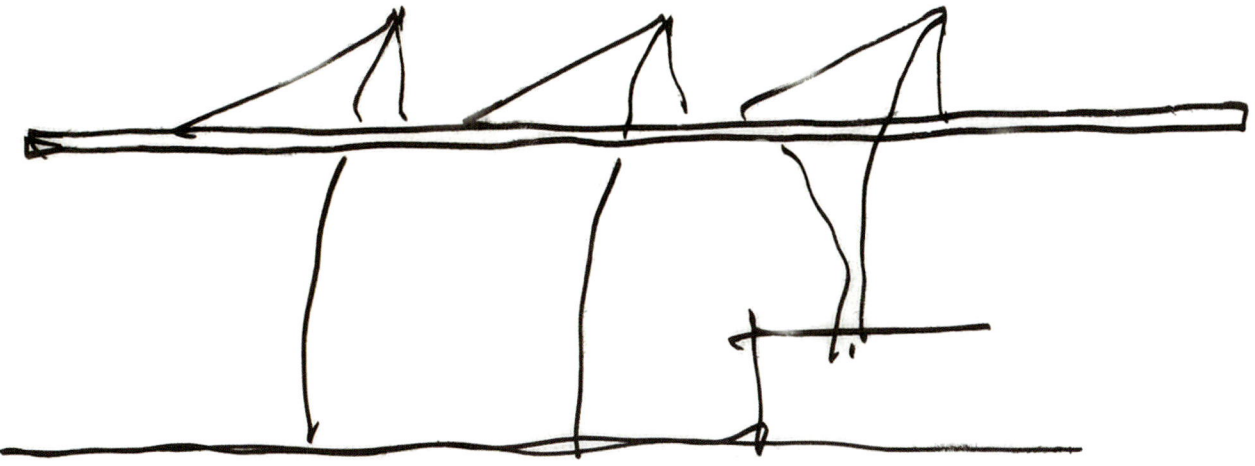

Tapered concrete columns are shaped like elegant blooming flowers, split down the middle to admit natural light and breezes from the pyramidal rooftop openings, whose checkered pattern is reminiscent of the Changhua rice paddies. The columns not only perform as light tubes, but also act as rain-water collectors for drainage. They are positioned alongside the main circulation route, with the result that passengers on the escalators can seem to appear and disappear in succession when viewed from the concourse. This adds a playful edge to a space already enlivened with multiple plantings, ensuring that waiting for a high-speed train that only stops here once an hour is no longer dull and tiring.

Slender poles support the canopy that shades the waiting area outside a double-height concourse, which opens up to the environment through a cable-braced glass curtain wall. Restaurants and services are located on the ground floor, and tickets are checked on the mezzanine level, from where travelers can ascend to either side of the elevated tracks. Graceful Y-columns hold up the tilted metal canopies that shelter the platforms and passengers from unpleasant weather.

▶ Tapered concrete columns draw in natural light to illuminate the double-height concourse.

Sectional perspective through the concourse, the ticket area, and the elevated platforms.

The station is a symbolic bridge between the slow-paced routines of agriculture and the rapid motion of trains whizzing past. Its lithe structural aesthetic gives the building a graceful bearing, while the botanical embellishments soften the defined edges of synthetic materials. The plantings extend to the waiting and parking areas, carrying on the fusion of the fast and the slow, the soft and the hard, established by this oasis of serenity, linked visually to the landscape yet segregated within its glass cocoon.

HOTEL RESONANCE TAIPEI

Completed year: 2019 | Location: Taipei, Taiwan

Client: Fubon Life Insurance Co., Ltd.
Area: 18,711 m²

The Hotel Resonance Taipei inhabits a long and narrow corner site with a slender slab of guest rooms running east to west. Its architectural language allows for multiple interpretations. It could be seen as resembling a giant game of Jenga in progress, with various blocks part-removed from the stack. It could also be an enormous chest of drawers—with some drawers left half-open. Alternatively, the culture writer Dan Q. Dao, writing in Time Magazine, observed that the facade seemed to have been "designed to evoke frames on a film roll."

In keeping with the latter interpretation, from the outside, each window offers the view of a scene played out by its room's occupants, featuring actors of all ages, ethnicities, and backgrounds. From the inside, each window offers a framed view of the outside world, as if projected onto a square screen. But whatever the interpretation, time froze before the Jenga player could remove their chosen block, before the drawers yielded what their owner was searching for, and before the film had the chance to start rolling.

'Another new arrival: Hilton's 175-room Hotel Resonance Taipei, which boasts a boxy black-and-white exterior designed to evoke frames on a film roll.'

- Dao, Dan Q. "World's Greatest Places 2021-Taipei." Time Magazine, 2021

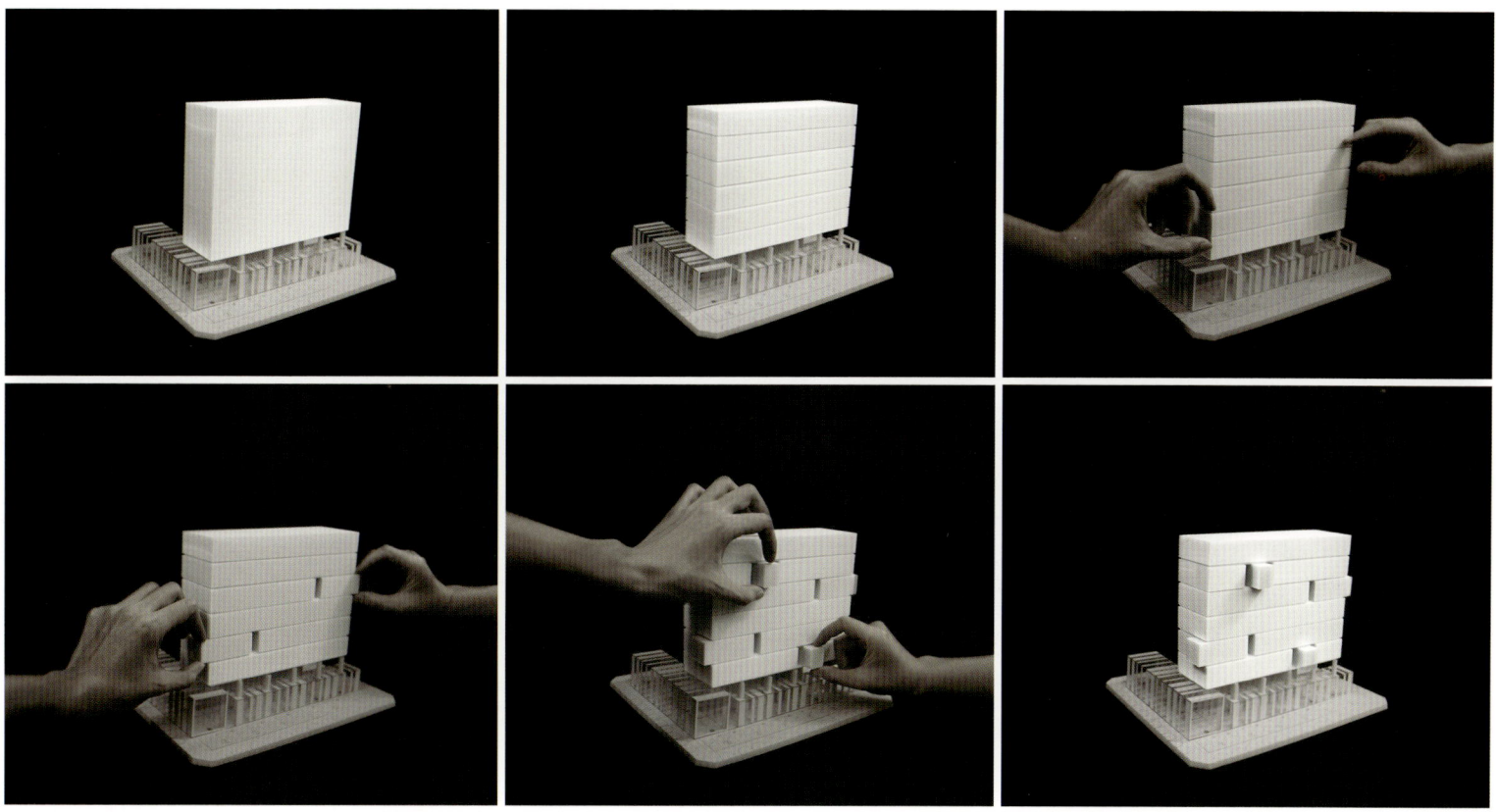

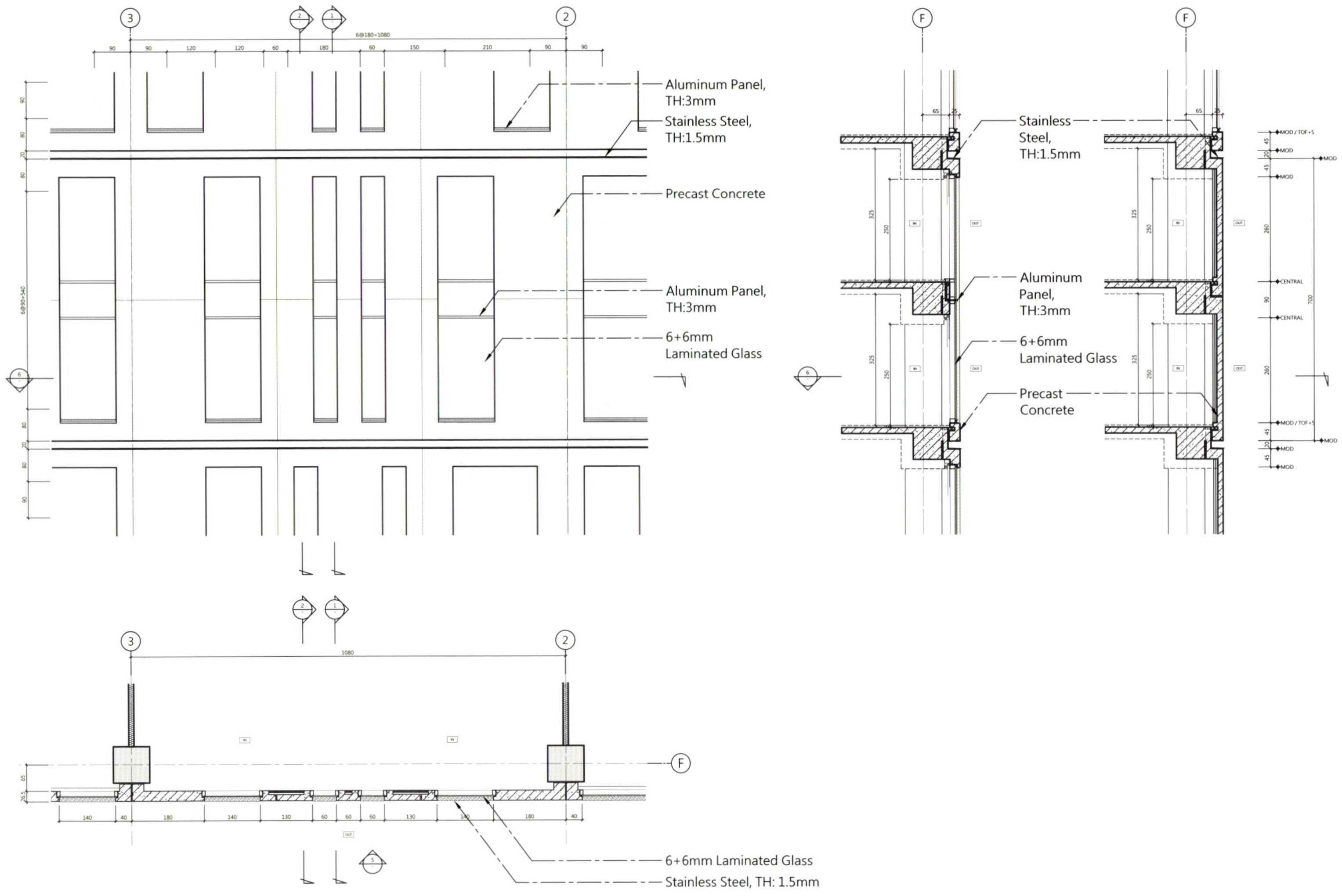

260 HOTEL RESONANCE TAIPEI

▲ TYPICAL WALL DETAIL

◀
Both wings were assembled with precast concrete blocks, which shortened the construction period by 11.5 months, while also greatly reducing waste, pollution, and impact on local traffic. The prefabricated elements came together perfectly due to the nature of the design —simple in massing yet intricate in detail.

▶
The north and south facades feature varied fenestration, with neatly laid out vertical slits of different widths; the shorter ends to east and west have oversized square windows, the most prominent being the projecting bay over the entry, which was originally intended to serve as a gallery.

The program of spaces is arranged in a logical progression, taking visitors on a journey from public to private as they travel from outside to inside, then from lower to upper floors. The first story, at one end of the spectrum, hosts public spaces that provide generous volumes for congregating and entertaining. The second story, in the middle of the scale, carries a range of hotel amenities for guests. The third story and above, at the opposite end of the spectrum, offer utter privacy, with 175 guest rooms that are compact and economical, to keep costs down for business travelers.

Hotel Resonance Taipei offers a quiet oasis in a busy district, full of heavy traffic and populated by educational and administrative institutions. The hotel is in the middle of a worn-down residential area, but although its elegance is unexpected in this setting, it sits comfortably next to its neighbors. Making clever and inventive use of its confined site, it serves as a convenient and welcome amenity for travelers, and for passing local residents who are drawn to its tranquility and persuaded to pause a while.

HAN-GU VILLA

Completed year: 2015 | Location: Beijing, China

HAN-GU VILLA

Client: China CYTS Tours Holding Co., Ltd.
Area: 10,237 m²

This 72-room resort is nestled in a valley below the Simatai Great Wall. Grouped in eight clusters of "stilt-houses," the accommodation spans 600 meters east to west. The buildings are connected by an open elevated footbridge that weaves between the trees, offering guests shifting views of the valley and mountains with every step, and allowing them to enjoy the harmonious coexistence of the manmade with the natural. At the western end, a reception hall serves as the threshold between public and private, restricting access to staff and guests only in order to guarantee a secure, high-end experience.

The building facades were constructed from environmentally friendly composite wood with a fine surface grain. Their colors blend perfectly with the setting, and their subtle tonal variations reflect the shifting colors of the surrounding landscape through different seasons and weather conditions.

▲
This luxury resort is located in a beautiful winding valley below the Simatai Great Wall—a natural setting that the architect pledged to protect upon first setting foot on the site.

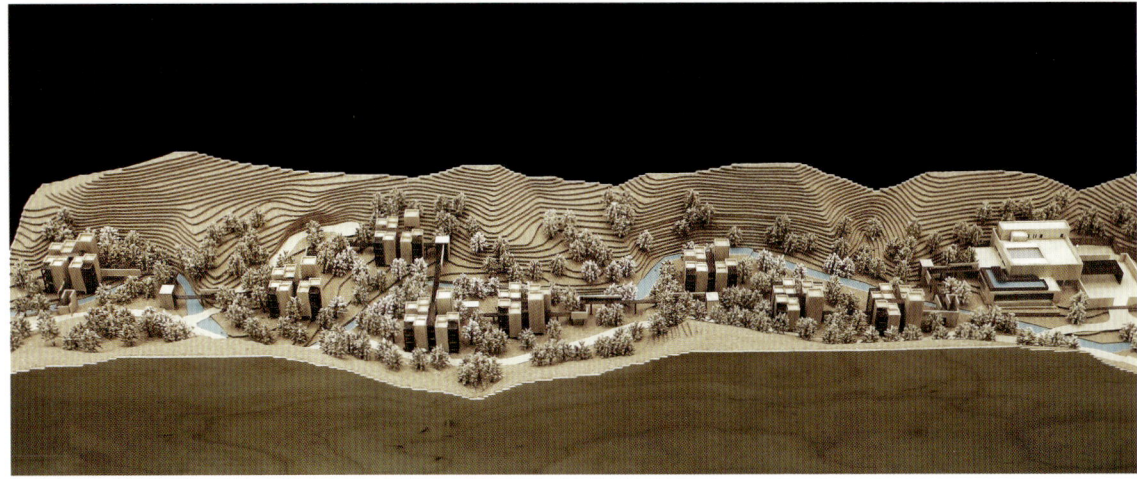

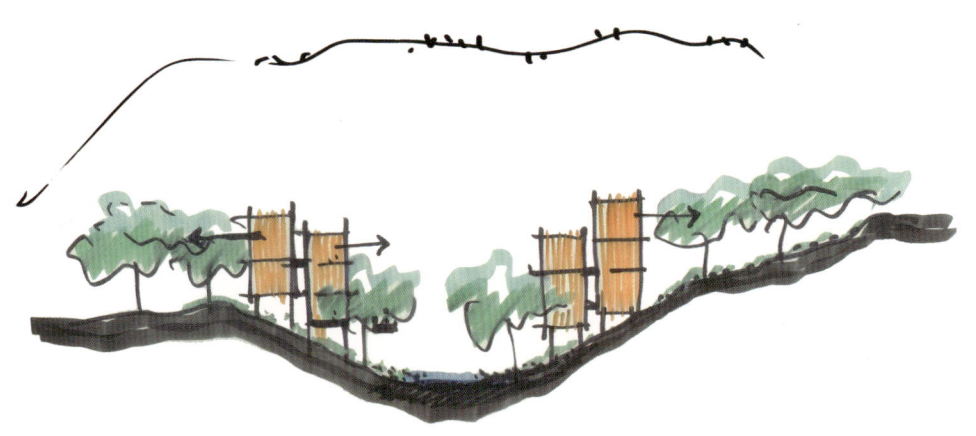

▶ A sketch showing the stilt-house concept, which minimized site grading and preserved as much vegetation as possible.

▲
The color of the composite wood blends perfectly with the context, as if the resort is camouflaged in the trees.

Han-Gu Villa tiptoes its way across the valley, careful not to intrude on the natural habitat. It arrived as a fabricated interpretation of its indigenous neighbors, and was arranged in the style of a settlement, with each cluster reminiscent of the vernacular cabin of early forest inhabitants. The rooms and the walkway hover gracefully above the stream and rocks, providing visitors an opportunity to appreciate and immerse themselves in nature, while causing minimal disruption to its growth.

HOTEL INDIGO TAIPEI

Completed year: 2019   Location: Taipei, Taiwan

Client: Esse Commerce Development Inc.
Area: 30,329 m²

Hotel Indigo is a hotel and retail complex in Taipei's recently developed Dazhi neighborhood, composed of a three-story crescent podium with a 12-story horseshoe extrusion. Retail stores fill the former, while bedroom units and hotel functions are packed into the latter. Shoppers and hotel guests enter via separate entrances in the podium, where the interior colors extend from the hotel lobby to the amenities space on Level 4. The hotel elevator opens up to a grand view of the outdoor roof garden, and dining facilities stretch out into both wings of the horseshoe. The building's layout was tailored to the irregular, fan-shaped site, aligning hotel corridors in an optimal circulatory arrangement. This arcing plan allows for a flexible layout over the entire width of the site and creates wide-angle views from the guest rooms.

The conch-like form derives from the golden spiral, which ensures both a logarithmic geometry and an aesthetic principle. Its proportions, from massing to height, keep it at an ideal balance that enriches the site without overwhelming it.

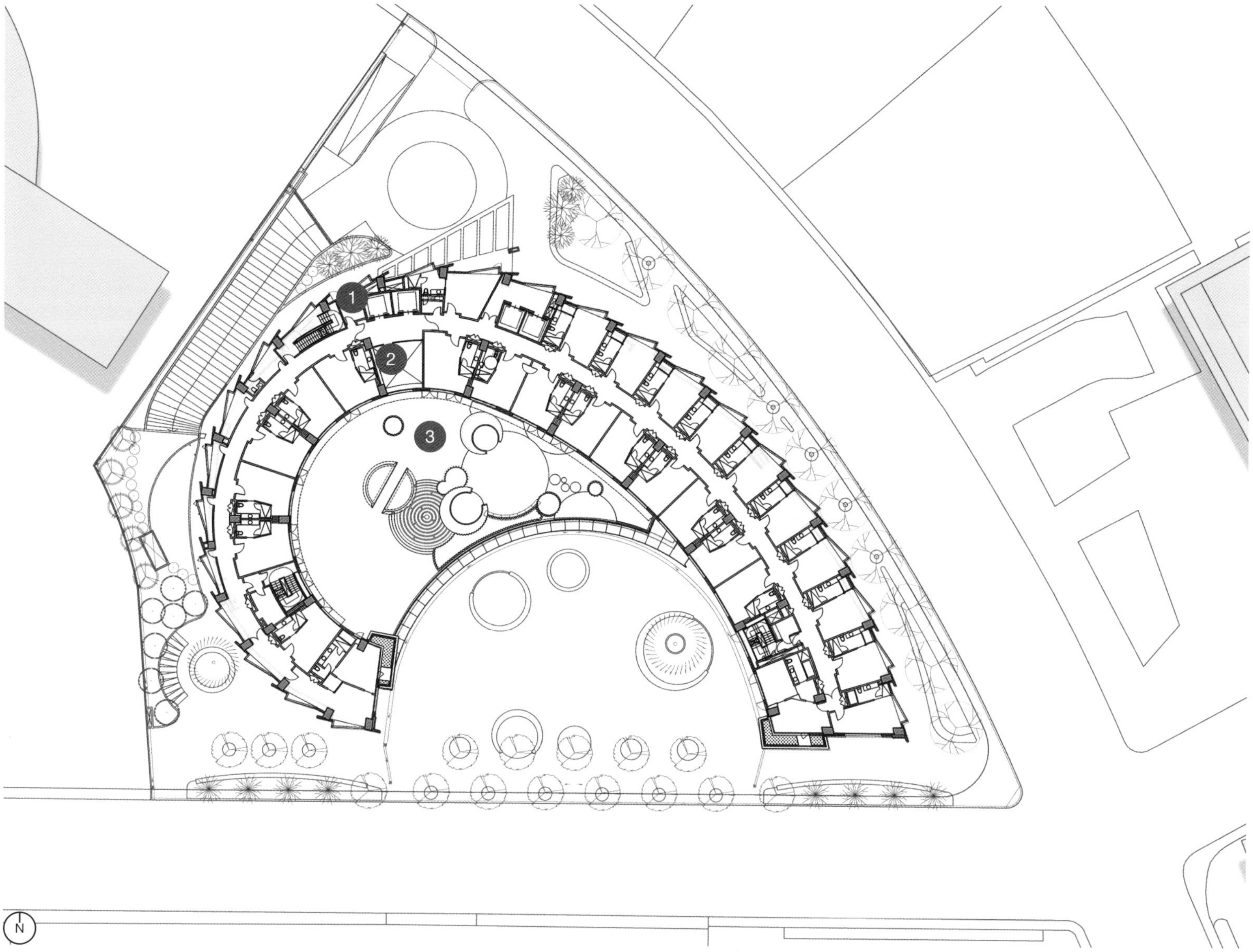

▲
TYPICAL FLOOR PLAN

1 Lift lobby
2 Terrace
3 Courtyard

▶ The initial inspiration for the hotel's design came from the kilns used by the brick and tile industries that once flourished along the Keelung River.

©Kevin Kelly, 1972

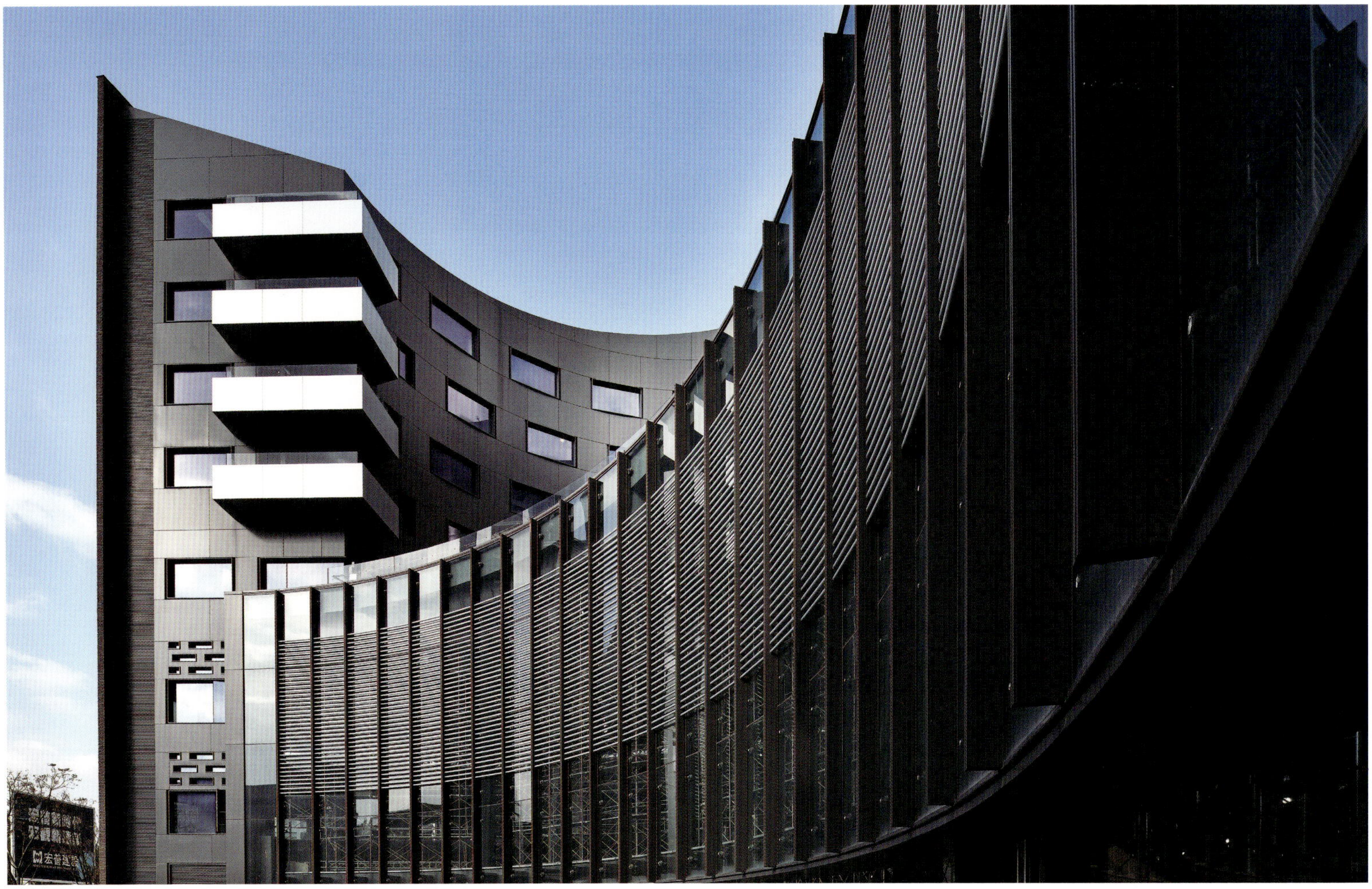

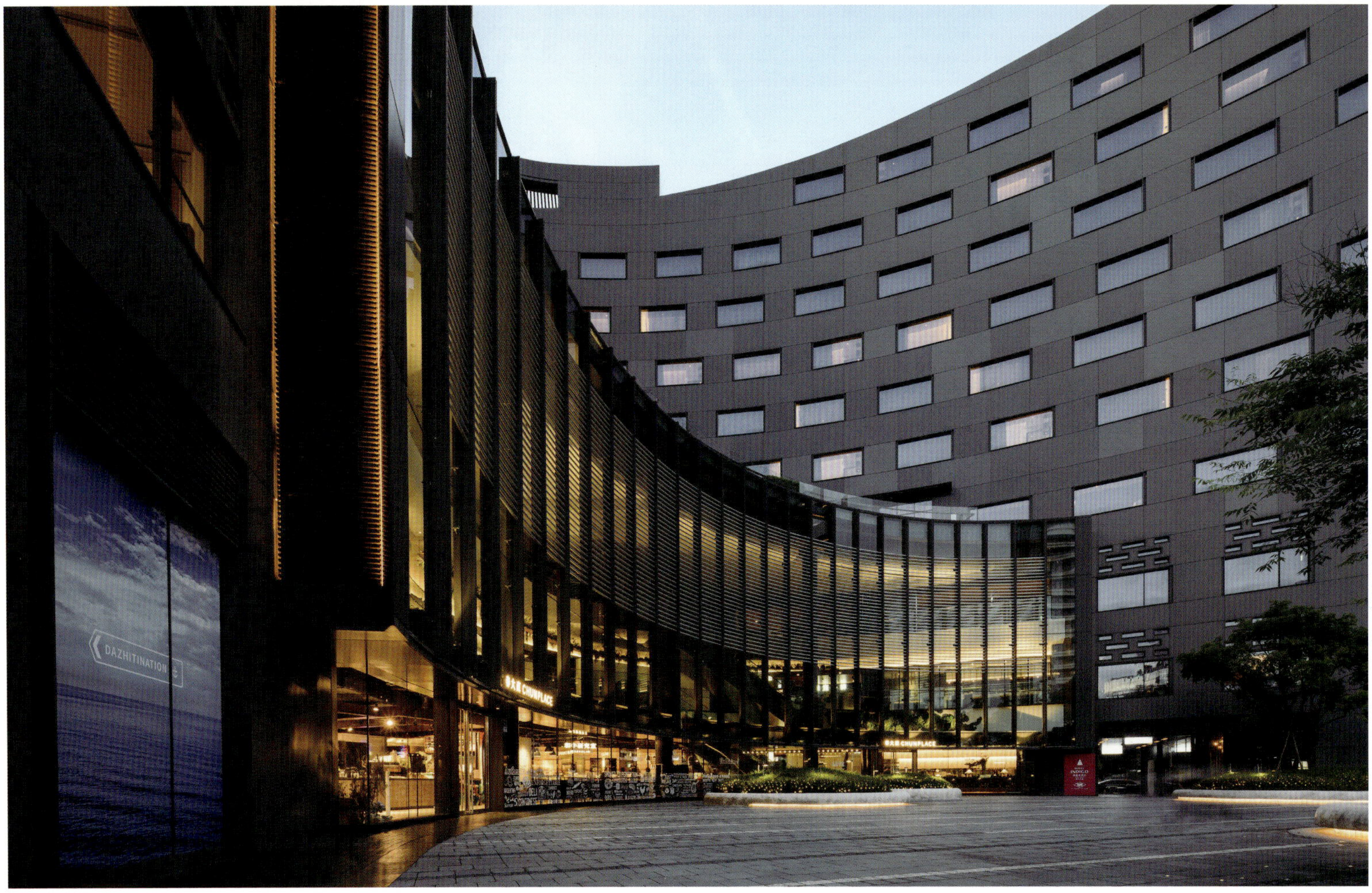

▶ The outer curve of the spiral on the north elevation is composed of 52,000 hand-split brick tiles to represent craftsmanship inherited from the past. The inner facade on the south elevation, made from glass curtain wall and aluminum panel sets with varying curvatures, symbolizes the technological advancements of the modern era.

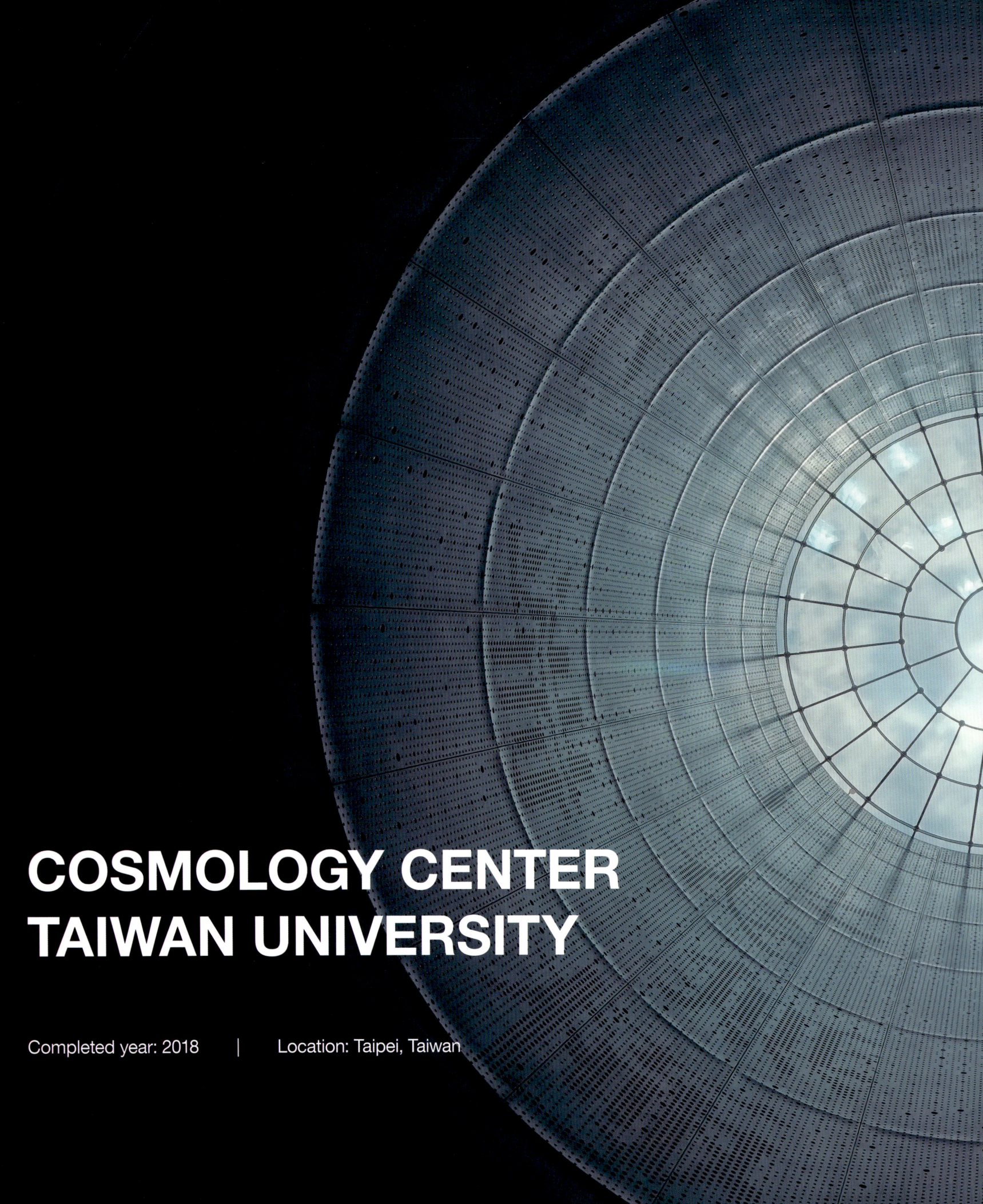

COSMOLOGY CENTER
TAIWAN UNIVERSITY

Completed year: 2018 | Location: Taipei, Taiwan

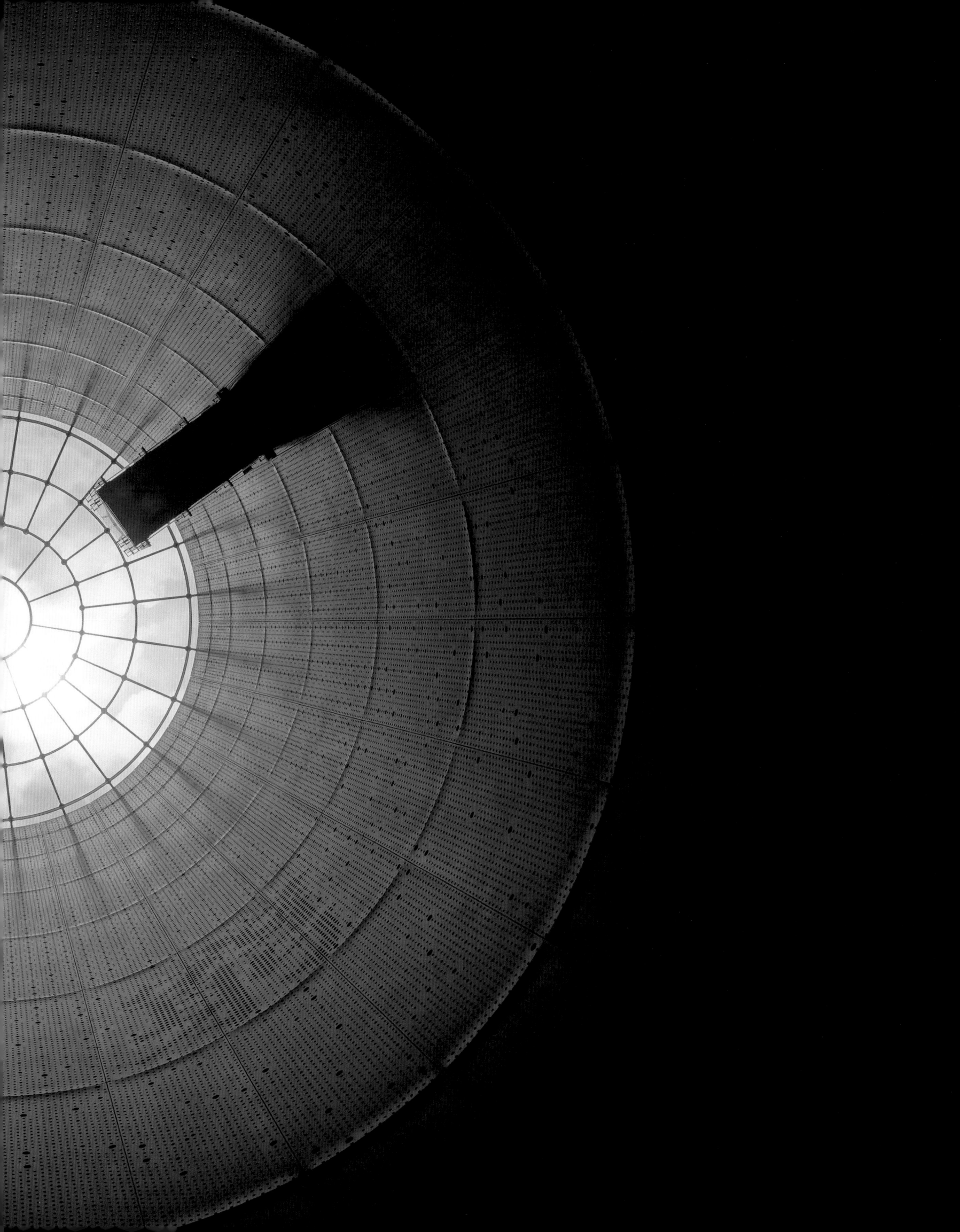

COSMOLOGY CENTER TAIWAN UNIVERSITY

Client: Chun Yee Cultural Foundation
Area: 10,980 m²

Primarily funded by a donation from the notable National Taiwan University (NTU) alumni Chee-Chun Leung, the Cosmology Center sits harmoniously within its environment. The subtle sphere within a cube reflects the ancient Chinese belief in a round heaven and a square earth, and perforated vertical louvers form a dynamic facade that both conceals and reveals the illusion of the sphere, depending on the angle from which the building is viewed. Inside, a rotunda floats in the center of the square plan, further underpinning the cosmological concepts that lie at the heart of the building. Moving about inside the center, students, teachers, and scientists are immersed in a spatial replica of their field of passion—in a design that was intended to inspire evolved analytical thinking, capable of challenging current ideas and pushing beyond boundaries.

The Cosmology Center stands tall and proud on the NTU campus, with the elevated Jianguo expressway to its north, and the beautiful Drunken Moon Lake to its south. The entrances of the building extend outward from a cross-shaped axis, drawing in like-minded individuals to gather at the central rotunda. To the east, the paving reaches into a previously existing park full of banyan trees, where the greenery creates a pleasant environment for relaxation.

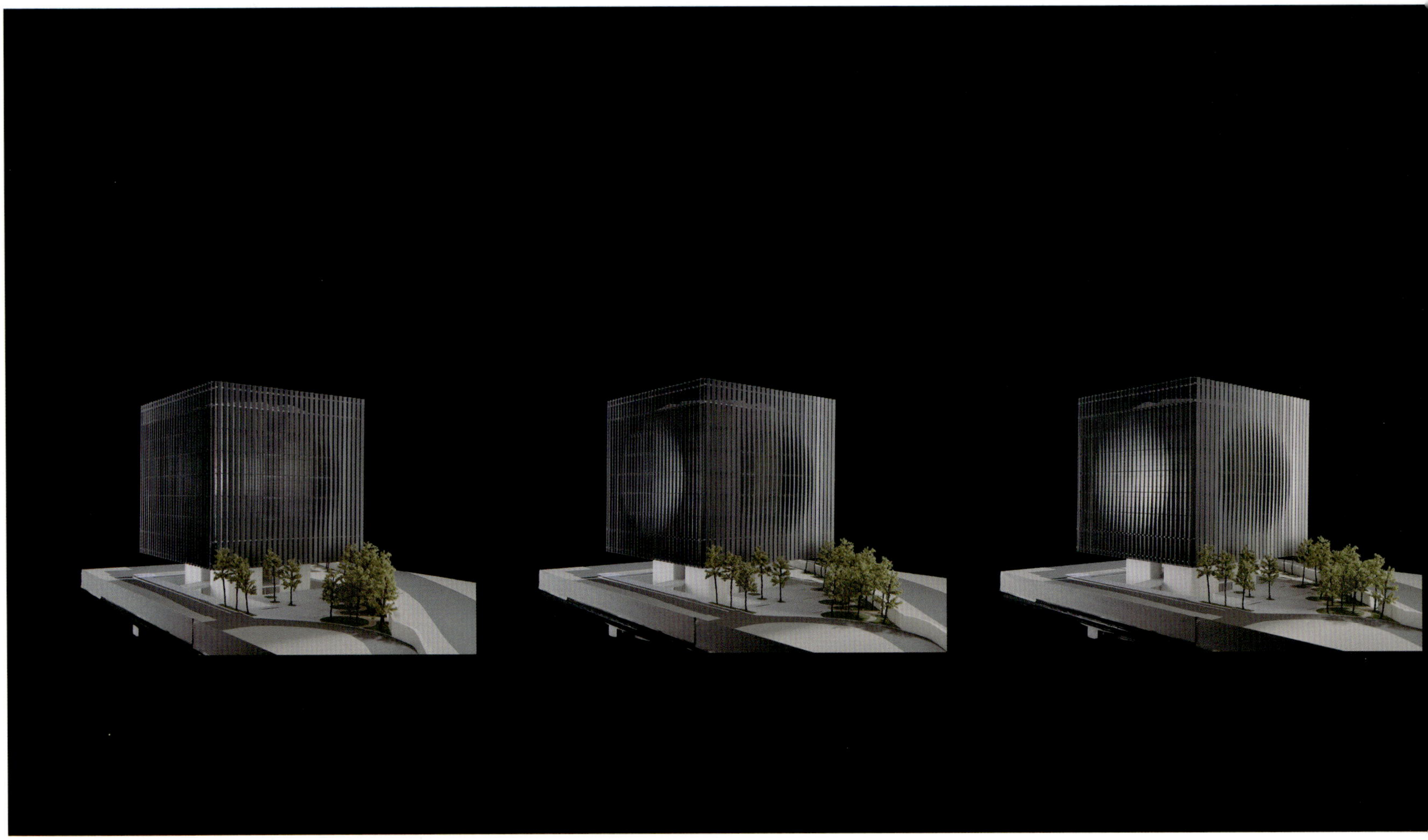

294 COSMOLOGY CENTER TAIWAN UNIVERSITY

▲
Slight variations in the depth of the louvers create the illusion of a white sphere within a black box, or vice versa, when viewed from different angles.

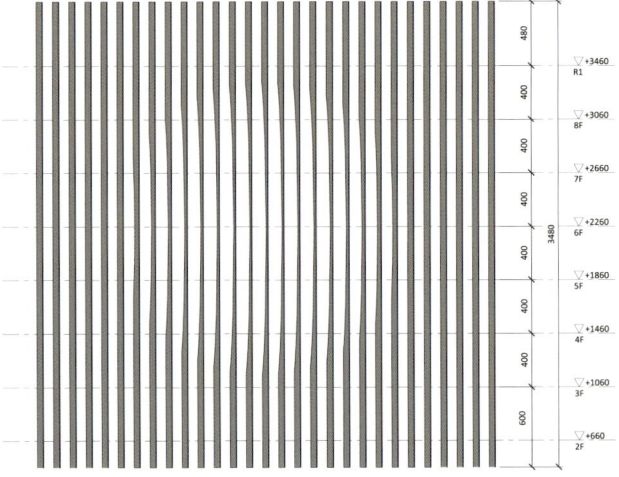

▲
EXTERNAL SUNSHADE ELEVATION

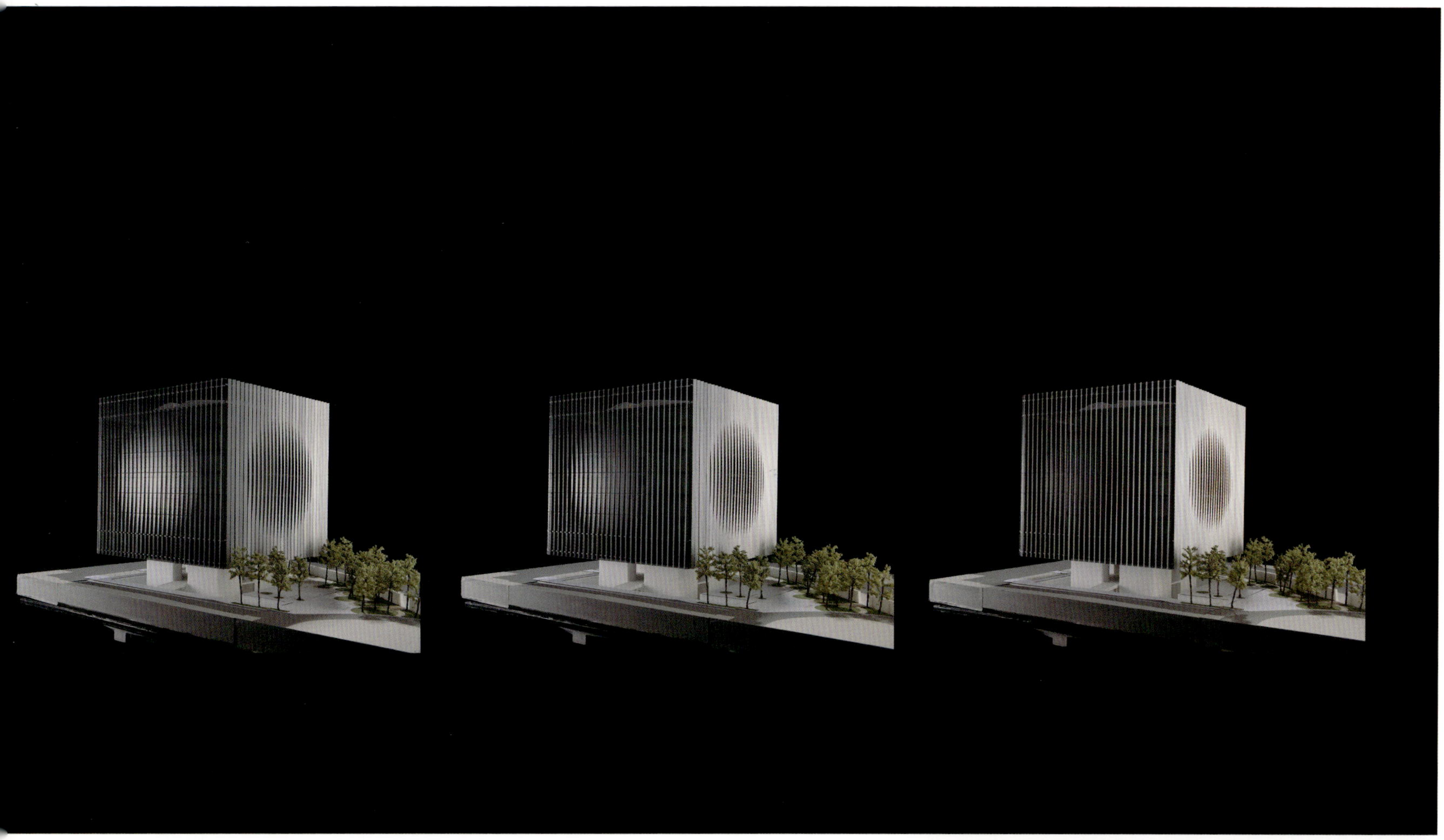

As a building that embodies traditional Chinese cosmology, the floating cube around a levitating sphere took form with the idea of challenging the force of gravity. A recessed concrete core takes on the primary structural load and stands firmly on a sunken courtyard, shaded by an overhanging cube that cantilevers out by seven meters. The notion of a harmonious "round" heaven, wrapped within a just "squared" earth, is realized both externally and internally. The perforated aluminum louvers that shade the glass curtain wall have depths that vary in a progressive sequence, which is what creates the illusion of a sphere inside the cube as the viewer moves around the dynamic, ever-changing facade.

296 COSMOLOGY CENTER TAIWAN UNIVERSITY

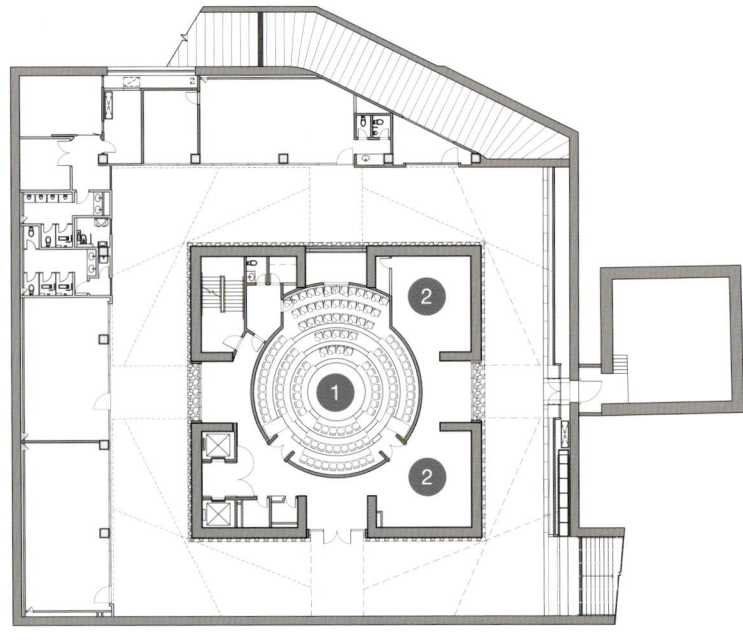

▲
BASEMENT FLOOR PLAN

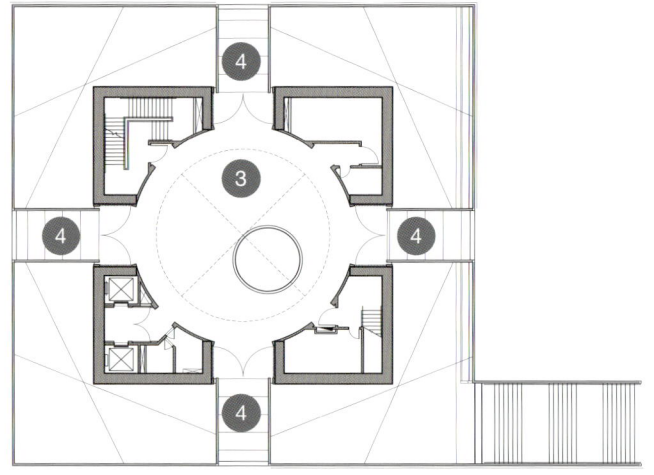

▲
GROUND FLOOR PLAN

1 Lecture hall
2 Exhibition
3 Atrium
4 Entrance
5 Lift lobby
6 Skylight

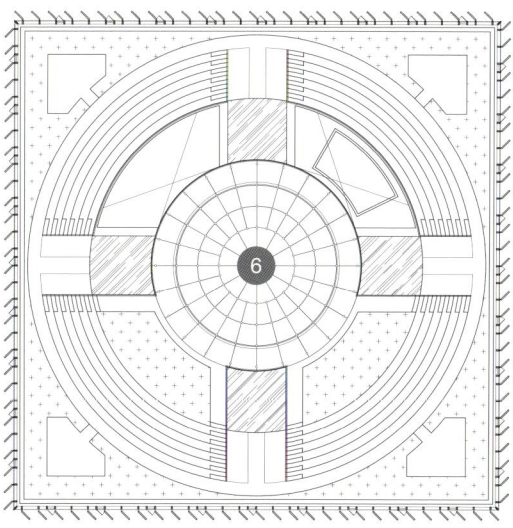

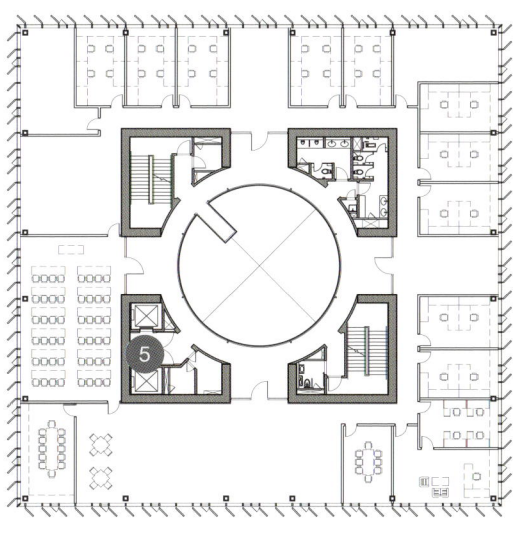
▲ TYPICAL FLOOR PLAN

▲ ROOF PLAN

Sectional perspective through the central atrium, the lab rooms, and the classrooms.

A few steps inside the building bring visitors to the tubular atrium that penetrates right up through the center. This is clad in perforated aluminum panels—yellow on the outside, dark blue on the inside, and featuring a prescient quote from the Han Dynasty astronomer and geographer Zhang Heng (78–139 CE): "Beyond all the observable there remains a vast unknown … Space has no bounds and time has no end." The rotunda is a tribute to that of the Pantheon in Rome, with an Oriental twist. Its 38-meter height intentionally matches that of the Pantheon, with a circular skylight in place of the Roman temple's oculus. Standing at the base of this cylindrical space, one gets a sense of the immensity of the cosmos, as the blue metal skin appears to soar up into an endless unknown. Circular perforations of different diameters create the effect of stars and galaxies in the night sky, and the sound-absorbing qualities of these openings give the space a sense of mystery and serenity.

These perforations allow natural light to filter into the corridors that encircle the atrium from Levels 2 to 8, casting a pattern of luminous dots that enliven the passage of scientists as they walk to their laboratories. These openings also indirectly reveal to inhabitants the time of day and weather conditions outside, like a scaled-down parallel universe that works simultaneously with, yet independently of, its real-world counterpart. On June 21, 2020, the center hosted an event that left witnesses in awe, as a once-in-a-century annular solar eclipse was replicated by each of the circular openings in the perforated panels, casting tens of thousands of silhouetted eclipses onto the floor and walls beyond.

Annular Solar Eclipse 2020.06.21

Annular Solar Eclipse 2020.06.21

HUPAN CENTER

Completed year: 2020 | Location: Hangzhou, China

©ALIBABA-JUN JIE SHEN

HUPAN CENTER

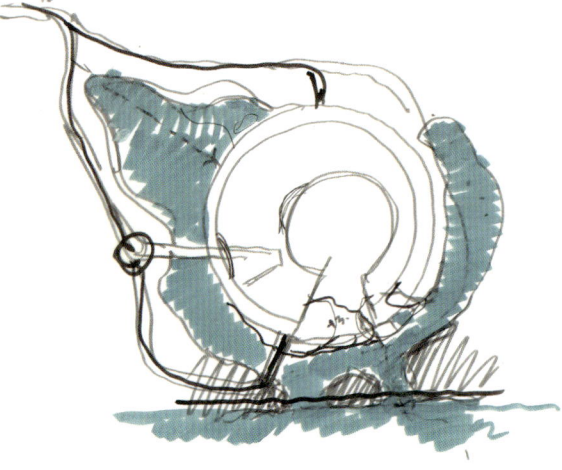

Client: Hupan Learning and Research Center of Entrepreneurship
Area: 43,814 m²

Hupan Center is a business and research center founded by nine celebrated Chinese entrepreneurs and scholars, with the goal of infusing graduates with a lively start-up spirit. The new campus is located in the Yuhang district of Hangzhou, Zhejiang province, and sits on a site bordered by water on three sides. It was conceived as a contemporary version of a traditional

Chinese garden, enclosed within a ring-like building, 160 meters in diameter and three stories in height, where occupants and visitors can share ideas, cherish traditions, and embrace new concepts.

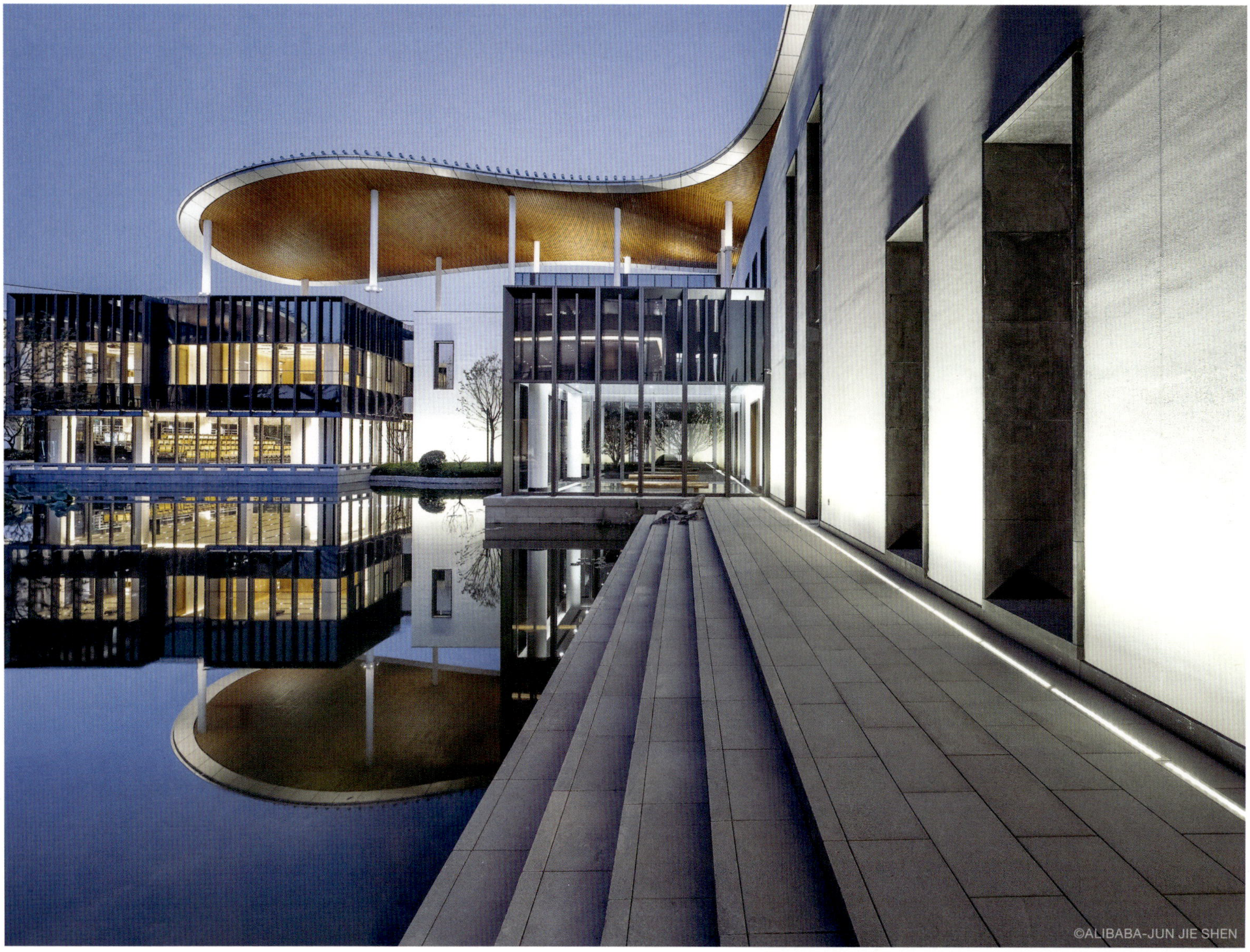

©ALIBABA-JUN JIE SHEN

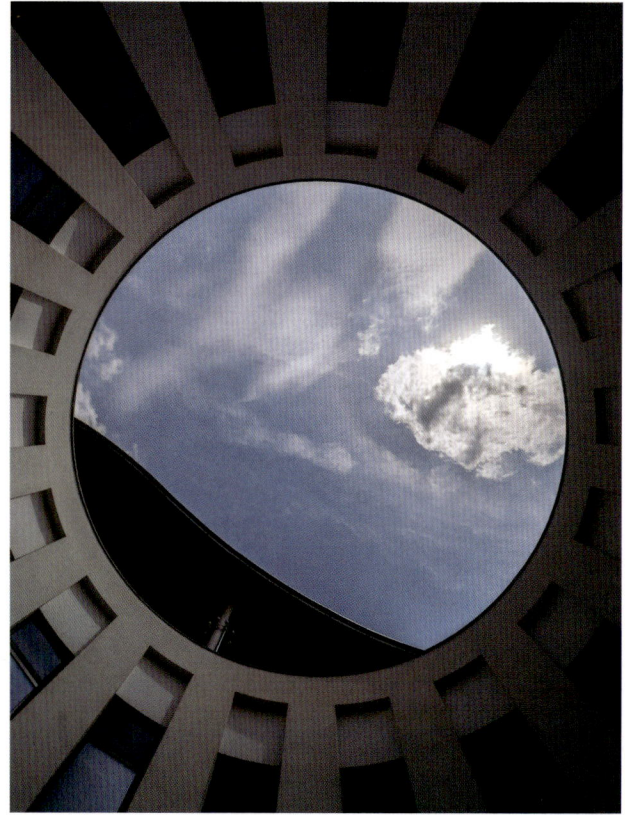

With the main service route to the north, the complex is entered from a bridge on the west side. Rows of bamboo line either side of the entrance plaza, welcoming visitors and employees into a realm of Oriental architecture that's very different to that of its surroundings. Shared facilities, including multipurpose halls of varying sizes, a small theater, stepped lecture rooms, and a canteen are deployed around the inner garden and lake. Most have expansive windows overlooking the central courtyard to establish visual connections between occupants in different parts of the campus. The administrative offices, study halls, and other service facilities, which require greater focus, are located in the quieter southeast corner and outer ring areas.

©ALIBABA-LYU CHENG

The organic, cloudlike roofs are a unique architectural component, and these provided an interesting challenge during the construction stage. The three silvery metal canopies are supported on slender poles, and together they form a total area of around 4,600 square meters. They shade a series of passageways and gathering spaces for social and pedagogical activities, and they offer a naturally ventilated zone safe from intense weather conditions. The canopies are finished on the underside with bamboo slats, which not only provide some warmth in these rooftop areas, but together with the building's simple white-washed walls and gray tiles, acknowledge the color palette and materials of traditional Chinese architecture.

DHARMA DRUM
INSTITUTE OF LIBERAL ARTS

Completed year: 2015 | Location: New Taipei, Taiwan

Client: Dharma Drum Institute of Liberal Arts (DILA)
Area: 42,457 m²

Master Sheng Yen, founder of the Dharma Drum Institute of Liberal Arts, issued three instructions for the creation of this build. First, he specified, the project needed to preserve the appearance of the existing terrain; second, the buildings needed to appear as if they had grown out of the site; and third, the overall style had to be one of timeless grandeur, ensuring that upon completion the buildings would have no jarring, novel elements, and able to retain their features for many decades to come. In response to the brief, KYA decided to hide all retaining walls behind a series of recessing platforms. The platforms are connected both internally and externally by 1,590 steps, which traverse between the varying elevations of this mountainside site.

The project uses enduring materials like architectural concrete, titanium-zinc panels, pebbledash walls, and timber to embody an architectural style that does not belong to any particular era. The buildings are also mostly low-rise structures that lean against the natural terrain, appearing, as requested, as if they are emerging out of the mountain itself. This decision also helped to minimize the need for excavation. The grand staircase rests comfortably on the slope of the site, and planting on the roofs and terraces extends its vegetation. The exterior and the interior, the natural and the built, the solids and the voids are all integrated to construct a series of interconnected theatrical spaces, where students and teachers roam freely, from one scene to another.

Sandwiched between the academic buildings and the living and recreational quarters, a 108-meter bridge spans the existing pond at the center of the site. Differing in structure from ordinary bridges, here the box girders were placed on one side of the bridge, freeing up the other side for viewing. Two round holes were then added at either end, highlighting the sudden change of scenery, and enhancing the shift in perspective that comes when walking across a bridge.

At present there are three buildings on campus: the Academic/Administration Building, the ChangYue College Dormitory, and the gymnasium. Architectural concrete was used throughout the former and the latter, creating an enduring and timeless style in keeping with Master Sheng Yen's vision. The ChangYue College Dormitory hosts the students' living quarters, and this is coated in pebbledash, creating a finish that is simple yet detailed in texture, and economical yet more than adequate in terms of quality.

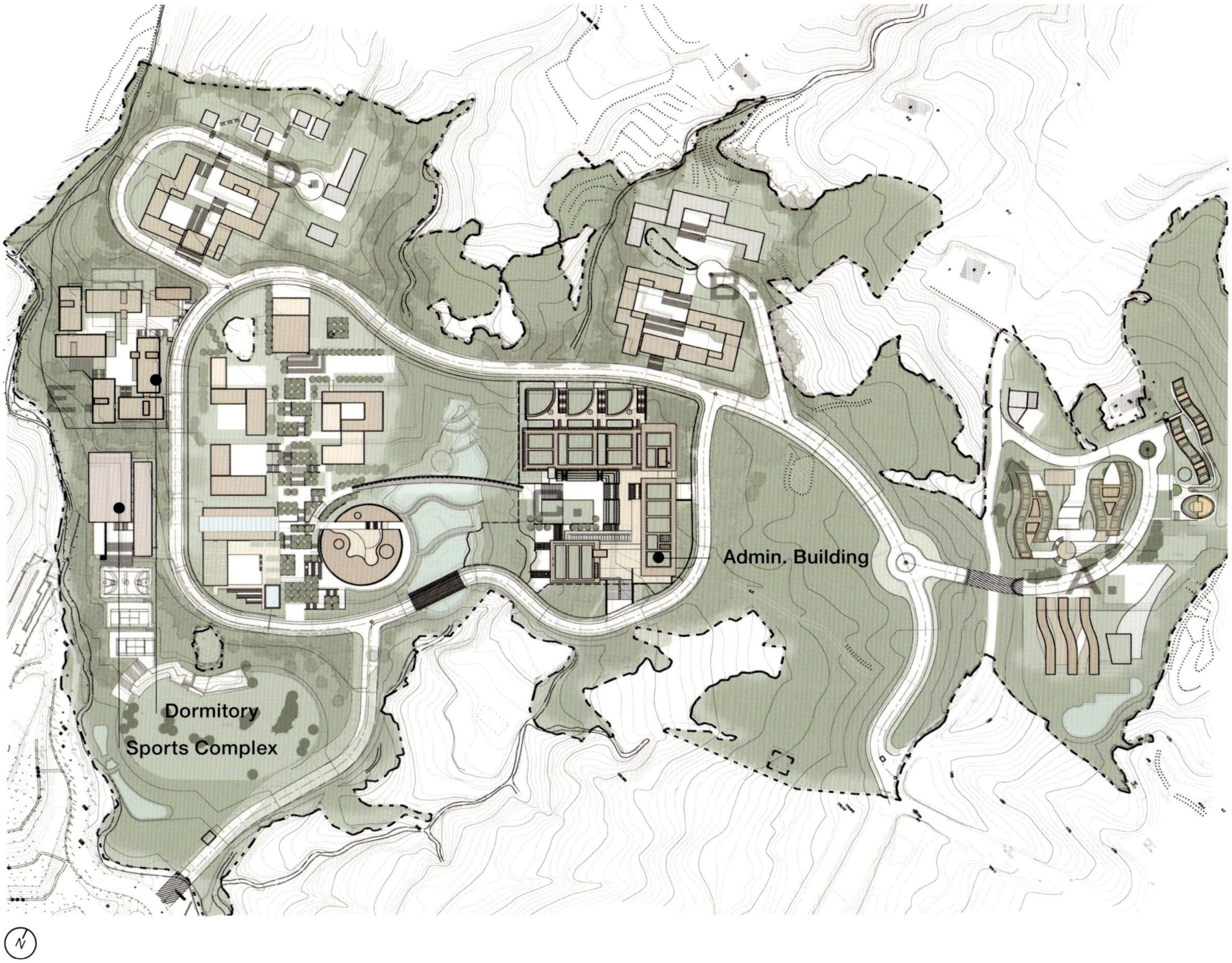

▲
SITE PLAN

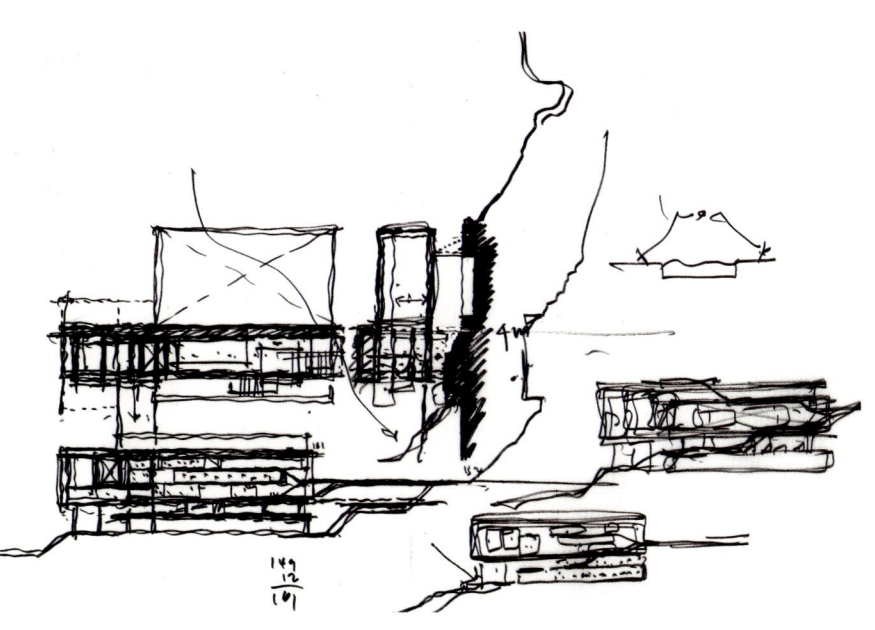

◀
The wide use of concrete embodies an architectural style of timeless grandeur, belonging not to a particular era and appearing unaffected by time for many decades to come.

Long sectional perspective through the lecture halls (left) and the canteen (right).

Sectional perspective through the dormitory.

◀
Volumes protrude outward to create additional viewing platforms over the mountains.

The ChanYue College Dormitory consists of six residence halls and one communal building. Following the slope of the terrain, the roof of each hall steps down one level from north to south to increase visual interest and lessen any sense of compression. The use of a timber balustrade introduces some warmth to these pebbledash buildings, and the setback balconies create a spatial depth that enriches the facade.

The main campus building is divided into three parts—the administrative building, the academy, and the activity center, with each occupying a side of the U-shaped plan. Keeping to the elevation of the surrounding landscape, the roof steps down to create staggered terraces for socializing or meditating. The horizontal layout of the three buildings fosters continuous circulation between balconies, corridors, bridges, and interior spaces at various levels. In a region that sees a lot of wet weather, students and staff are free to go about their business, protected by constant cover above their heads. In addition to creating sheltered walkways, the protruding ceilings, walls, and floors also frame views of the beautiful landscape beyond.

The gymnasium is composed of a square and a rectangular mass. The former has a height of seven meters, leaving ample space for all sporting activities; the latter is a box-in-box configuration, which alternately protrudes in and out to frame views and create social spaces. Openings punctuate the roof to bring in sunlight for an interplay of light and shadow, and the design takes advantage of the sloping terrain to channel fresh air into the interior. Pleasant spots like these are dotted throughout, offering places for students and staff alike to relax or meditate.

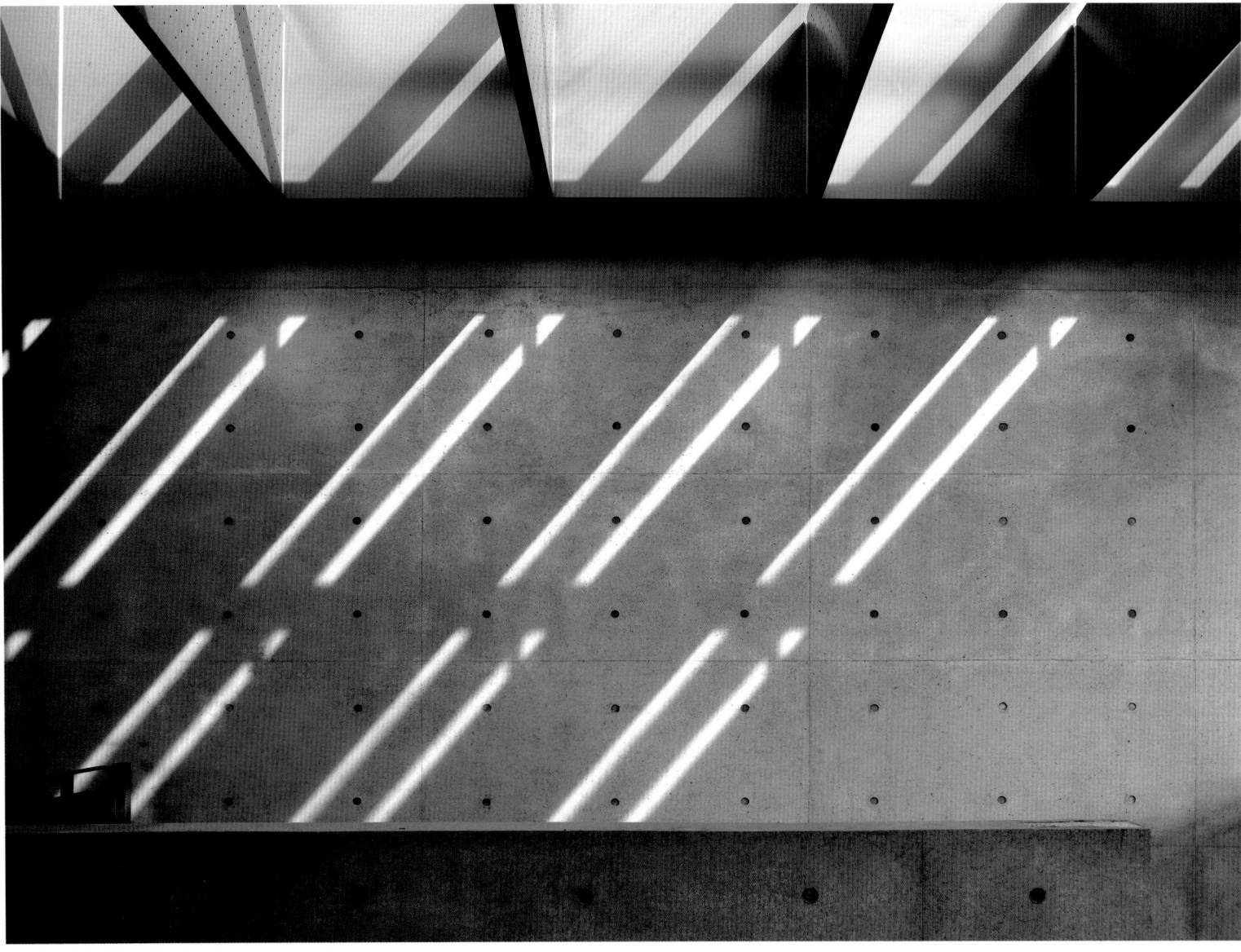

HAN PAO-TEH MEMORIAL MUSEUM

Completed year: 2022 | Location: Tainan, Taiwan

HAN PAO-TEH MEMORIAL MUSEUM

Client: Joseph ST Han and Karen Han
Area: 690 m²

Han Pao-Teh is widely recognized as one of the seminal figures of modern architectural theory in Taiwan. In honor of his work and contributions in the arts field, a memorial hall at the Tainan University of the Arts—an educational institution established by Han himself—was established to house and display his collections. As an embodiment of Han's attitude toward museums and the value of education, the hall unites seamlessly with the exhibition and teaching spaces.

Adhering to the concept of a "cube within a cube," the geometric simplicity of the hall's configuration underpins the themes that inspired it: Multiple faces signify the many aspects of Han's expertise, while the robust quality established with the use of architectural concrete pays homage to his indomitable spirit.

In terms of spatial arrangements, an entrance pond separates two arrival routes—a ramp on the left, which descends gradually to the ground floor, and a stairway on the right, which ascends to the second floor. The latter brings visitors into the main student exhibition space—an impressive cubic space, 13.5 meters tall, and pleasantly intruded upon by an imposing cubic mass, as if untouched by the laws of gravity. The floating cube holds the Han Pao-Teh Exhibition Room, a two-story, auditorium-like space that protrudes diagonally from the larger cube. The rotated cube also creates a split in the wall, allowing a strong shaft of light to enter, the sharp contrast between light and shadow creating a dramatic atmosphere in the interior.

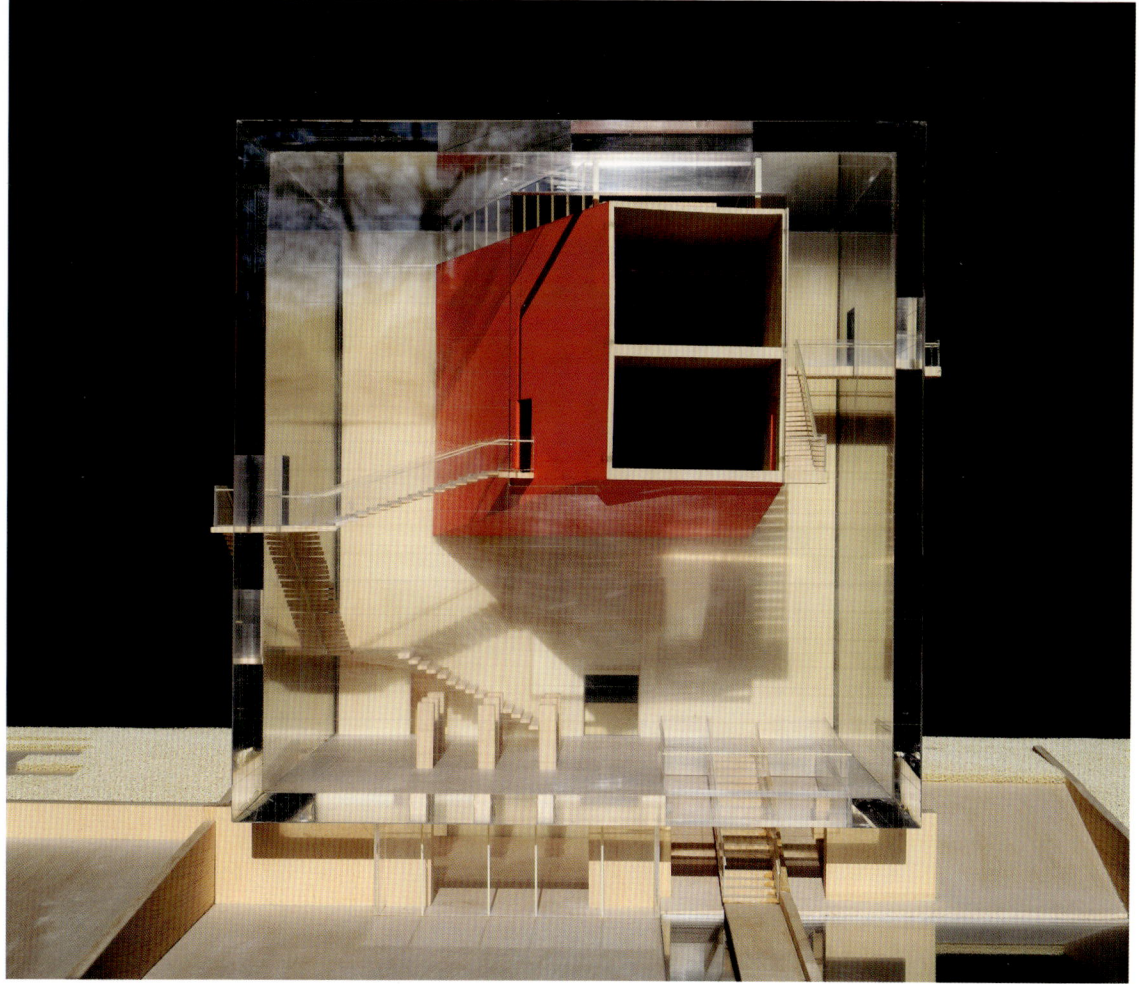

▲
The work from the same hands, 26 years apart, sits side by side with Han Pao-Teh Memorial Hall (2022) to the left and the TNNUA College of Sound and Image Arts (1996) to the right.

The spaces are tied together by a theatrical staircase that travels between the interior and exterior, taking visitors on an ascending counterclockwise journey, as if rewinding the clock back to Han's lifetime. Perhaps some will be enlightened by the shift in paradigm, or experience a cultural awakening along the way.

This memorial pays homage to Han Pao-Teh himself, and to his remarkable contribution to Taiwanese culture and education, in the field of architecture and the arts in general.

Note:
Han Pao-Teh (1934–2014) played a significant role in Kris Yao's architectural education, as his teacher and mentor. In 2015, Han's family commissioned Yao to design the Han Pao-Teh Memorial Museum for the Tainan University of the Arts campus. Han was heavily involved in the design and founding of the university, and he also became its first superintendent.

SELECTED PROJECTS

1 Xiang Guang Shan Temple
1995 - 1998
Location: Taichung, Taiwan

2 Yuan Ze University Library
1995 - 1998
Location: Taoyuan , Taiwan

3 Continental Engineering Corporation Headquarters
1994 - 1999
Location: Taipei, Taiwan

4 TNNUA College of Sound and Image Arts
1996 - 1998
Location: Tainan, Taiwan

5 Tomihiro Art Museum Competition
2001 -
Location: Gunma Prefecture, Japan

6 **The Drape House**
2003 -
Location: Nanjing, China

7 **Palace Museum, Southern Branch-2004 International Competition**
2004 -
Location: Chiayi, Taiwan

8 **Quanta Research & Development Center**
2002 - 2005
Location: Taoyuan, Taiwan

9 **Hsinchu High Speed Rail Station**
2000 - 2006
Location: Hsinchu, Taiwan

10 **Taipei Fuhsing Private School**
2000 - 2007
Location: Taipei, Taiwan

11 **Fo Guang Shan Monastery, North Carolina**
2004 - 2008
Location: North Carolina, USA

1 Kelti Group Headquarters
2005 - 2009
Location: Taipei, Taiwan

2 Shih Chien University Gymnasium
2003 - 2009
Location: Taipei, Taiwan

3 Shih Chien University Library
2003 - 2009
Location: Taipei, Taiwan

4 Lanyang Museum
2000 - 2010
Location: Yilan, Taiwan

5 Fo Guang Shan Monastery, Vienna
2004 - 2010
Location: Vienna, Austria

6 Bhutan Shrine Paro
2008 - 2011
Location: Bhutan

7 China Steel Corporation Headquarters
2004 - 2012
Location: Kaohsiung, Taiwan

8 Fo Guang Shan Monastery, Bussy, France
2008 - 2012
Location: Paris, France

9 Luodong Government Center
2012 -
Location: Yilan, Taiwan

12 Wutaishan Retreat Center
2013 -
Location: Wutaishan, China

15 Eslite Suzhou
2009 - 2015
Location: Suzhou, China

1 WithIn · WithOut - KRIS YAO Selected Works Exhibition
2015 - 2016
Location: Shanghai, China

2 Shanghai Culture Center
2018 -
Location: Shanghai, China

3 NYCU Hospital
2019 -
Location: Hsinchu, Taiwan

4 Tianyige Museum
2019 -
Location: Zhejiang, China

5 Nanjing Shangqinhuai International Culture Exchange Center
2016 - 2020
Location: Nanjing, China

6 Xiamen Bank Headquarters
2020 -
Location: Xiamen, China

7 Shenzhen Natural History Museum Competition
2020 -
Location: Shenzhen, China

8 Shenzhen International Performance Center Competition
2020 -
Location: Shenzhen, China

9 S'Young Park
2021 -
Location: Hunan, China

10 Sunbrid Residence
2021 -
Location: Taoyuan, Taiwan

11 Compal World Headquarters Competition
2021 -
Location: Taipei, Taiwan

12 Tokyo Electron Limited Tainan Office
2021 -
Location: Tainan, Taiwan

13 Dzongsar Museum
2016 - 2022
Location: Sichuan, China

14 Kinmen County Central Library and Art Museum Competition
2022 -
Location: Kinmen, Taiwan

15 Jiang Ning Art Museum
2016 - 2023
Location: Nanjing, China

TEAM

SECTION
KRIS YAO | ARTECH

CREDITS & GRATITUDE

I would like to take this opportunity to express gratitude to all who has worked on the birth of this monograph and those who had taken part in the projects within. I would particularly like to thank Ying Jung Lu and Hsin Chun Huang for their creative minds behind the design, layout, and cover of this monograph. I also thank Xiang Jen Yao, Grace Lin, Ping Chiao for their leadership; Michael Webb, Nini Lee, Angela Koo, and Robert Hall for all text-related works; Doris Chen and Davina Lin for graphic edits and assistance throughout the course of the preparation of this book; and finally, Maria Lezhnina, Chi-Kuei Chiu, Yen-Ting Chen, Ming-Xiao Lin, and Winnie Wang for the sectional perspectives of the projects.

Finally, I want to thank all the colleagues of **KRIS YAO | ARTECH**, past and present. Their individual and collective contributions to the art of building can never be sufficiently recognized.

Kris Yao, Hon. FAIA
Founder

Conceived by **Kris Yao, Hon. FAIA**

Editorial management by **Xiang Jen Yao**

Design, layout, and cover by **Ying Jung Lu** and **Hsin Chun Huang**

Foreword by **Michael Webb**

Project texts and captions by **Nini Lee** and **Angela Koo**

Translation consulted by **Robert Hall**

Graphics by **Davina Lin** and **Doris Chen**

Photographs and visualizations by **5foreststudio, ALIBABA-JUN JIE SHEN, ALIBABA-LYU CHENG, Bian Jie, Bota, Chao Yu Chen, Chih Yen Tsai, Ching Kuang Liao, Chris Stowers, Chyuan Jen Chang, Chung-Min Lin, Commonwealth Publishing Group, David Chen, Dean Cheng, Fei-Chun Ying, Getty Images, GRANDJOY, Herry Lou, Hupan Learning and Research Center of Entrepreneurship, Hsiang-Yun Mai, Jack Ou, Jeffrey Cheng, KLOMFAR, Kris Provoost, KRIS YAO | ARTECH, Kyleyu Photo Studio, Liu Chen Hsiang, Marc Gerritsen, MLee Studio, Nanjing Daily Cui Xiao, Pay Tsung Pan, Ping Chiao, Shawn Liu Studio, Shephotoerd Co., Steve Lee, StudioSZ Photo, Taiwan Semiconductor Manufacturing Company, Ltd., Tom Hung, Tzu-Kang Huang, YHLAA, Yueh-Lun Tsai, Yu Tzu Chin, Wen Zhong Gao, Willy Berre, Wuzhen Tourism Co., Ltd., Zongsa Quba, ZOOMARCH**, USGBC® and the related logo are trademarks owned by the U.S. Green Building Council® and are used with permission.

ORO Editions
Publishers of Architecture, Art, and Design
Gordon Goff: Publisher

www.oroeditions.com
info@oroeditions.com

Published by ORO Editions

Copyright © 2024 **KRIS YAO | ARTECH**

All rights reserved. No part of this book may be reproduced, stored in a retrieval system, or transmitted in any form or by any means, including electronic, mechanical, photocopying of microfilming, recording, or otherwise (except that copying permitted by Sections 107 and 108 of the US Copyright Law and except by reviewers for the public press) without written permission from the publisher.

You must not circulate this book in any other binding or cover and you must impose this same condition on any acquirer.

Author: Kris Yao, Hon. FAIA
Book Design: Ying Jung Lu and Hsin Chun Huang
Project Manager: Jake Anderson

10 9 8 7 6 5 4 3 2 1 First Edition

ISBN: 978-1-954081-41-3

Color Separations and Printing: ORO Editions Inc.
Printed in Hong Kong, China

ORO Editions makes a continuous effort to minimize the overall carbon footprint of its publications. As part of this goal, ORO, in association with Global ReLeaf, arranges to plant trees to replace those used in the manufacturing of the paper produced for its books. Global ReLeaf is an international campaign run by American Forests, one of the world's oldest nonprofit conservation organizations. Global ReLeaf is American Forests' education and action program that helps individuals, organizations, agencies, and corporations improve the local and global environment by planting and caring for trees.

KRIS
YAO
ARTECH

姚仁喜
大元
建築工場